Dare to believe in the creativity, resilience, insight and faith of a singular peopl history—*and a singula*

> Waiting for the Messiah doesn't mean just sitti writing off the world as it is now. It doesn't me warfare or throwing off the shackles of socially acceptable behavior. And it doesn't necessarily mean envisioning acts of miraculous deliverance or heavenly rewards for the righteous.... Waiting for the Messiah means simply that we believe things will get better than this."
>
> —FROM THE INTRODUCTION

What does it mean to wait for the Messiah—a restoration of ancient Israel? A universal perfection of humanity by humanity? A time of warfare and fear? A totally altered universe?

Rabbi Elaine Rose Glickman explores these ancient messianic visions and others that developed over the three-thousand-year Jewish tradition of passion and patience. She shows that by understanding Judaism's relationship with the Messiah you can have deeper insight into the words of the prophets, the narratives of the Bible and the experience of Jewish people across generations. And as you acquaint yourself with who the Messiah traditionally is and what the Messianic Age traditionally means, you may find your soul stirring, in wakefulness, in recognition and maybe even in belief.

Truly unmatched in its range, scholarship and insight—and unique in its accessibility and engaging style—*The Messiah and the Jews* will capture your attention as you seek wisdom, wonder and—above all—hope.

"Drawing on Rabbi Glickman's well-ordered knowledge of the subject ... quickly moves beyond the historical or theological and into the spiritual. Shows how every Jew has a stake in the Messiah's coming."
—RABBI DAVID ROSEN, Congregation Beth Yeshurun, Houston, Texas

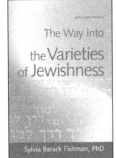
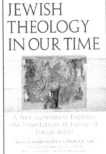

THE
Messiah
AND THE
Jews

Three Thousand Years
Tradition, Belief
of and Hope

RABBI ELAINE ROSE GLICKMAN

Foreword by Rabbi Neil Gillman, PhD
Preface by Rabbi Judith Z. Abrams, PhD

For People of All Faiths, All Backgrounds
JEWISH LIGHTS Publishing

The Messiah and the Jews:
Three Thousand Years of Tradition, Belief and Hope

© 2013 by Elaine Rose Glickman
Foreword © 2013 by Neil Gillman
Preface © 2013 by Judith Z. Abrams

Library of Congress Cataloging-in-Publication Data
Glickman, Elaine Rose.
  The Messiah and the Jews : three thousand years of tradition, belief, and hope / Rabbi Elaine Rose Glickman.
     pages cm
  Includes bibliographical references and index.
  ISBN 978-1-58023-690-4 (pbk)
  1. Messiah—Judaism. 2. Messianic era (Judaism) I. Title.
  BM615.G575 2013
  296.3'36—dc23

                                    2013002425

ISBN 978-1-68336-404-7 (hc)

Manufactured in the United States of America
Cover Design: Heather Pelham
Interior Design: Kelley Bureau

Published by Jewish Lights Publishing

www.jewishlights.com

For Brenner,
for Mo,
for Leo,
and for Eden

CONTENTS

Foreword   xi

Preface   xiii

Introduction   xvii

CHAPTER ONE
The Messiah Is Coming!   1

Where Is the Messiah Now?   2

When Will the Messiah Come?   4

Can We Make the Messiah Come Faster?   7

How Will the Messiah Appear?   10

Has the Messiah Been Revealed Before?   13

How Can We Recognize the True Messiah?   16

CHAPTER TWO
The Messiah Will Rule Over Israel   19

What Does "Messiah" Mean?   20

Why Must the Messiah Be Descended
from King David?   22

Why Do Messianic Hopes Focus on Israel?   25

What Is the "Ingathering of the Exiles"?   27

What Is the Relationship between
the State of Israel and the Messiah?   30

How Did the Messiah Become Associated
with Supernatural Elements?   33

CHAPTER THREE

The Messiah Is a Warrior 37

What Will the World Be Like Just Before
the Messiah Comes? 38

What Is Apocalyptic Literature? 41

Against Whom Will the Messiah Go to War? 44

Who Is the Messiah ben Joseph? 47

Who Is Hephzibah? 50

How Will the Messiah Triumph? 52

CHAPTER FOUR

The Messiah Will Change Everything 57

How Will the Natural World Be Different
in the Days of the Messiah? 58

What Will People Be Like in the Messianic Age? 61

What Will Society Be Like in the Messianic Age? 64

When the Messiah Is Here, How Will
Judaism Be Practiced? 66

What Is the Resurrection of the Dead? 70

What Is the Feast of the Righteous? 72

CHAPTER FIVE

The Messiah Will Establish God's Dominion 77

Who Is Elijah? 78

What Is the Role of the Shofar? 81

Will the Wicked Be Brought to Justice
in the Messianic Age? 84

Will Everyone Be Jewish in the Days of the Messiah? 87

How Will We Relate to God in the Messianic Age? 89

What Is the Connection between Individual
and Communal Redemption? 92

CHAPTER SIX

The Messiah Is Us   97

 Who Is the "Suffering Servant"?   98

 What Is the Role of the Messiah in Hasidic Judaism?   101

 Who Is Rabbi Schneerson?   104

 What Did Classical Reform Judaism Teach about the Messiah?   107

 What Does Modern Liberal Judaism Teach about the Messiah?   110

 Can We Experience the Messiah?   113

Author's Note   117

Notes   119

Suggestions for Further Reading   143

Index   148

FOREWORD

For reasons that are not totally clear, Jewish eschatology (the study of the end of days) is now in fashion once again. For decades now, Jewish theologians have been thinking about and teaching about the contours of Jewish speculation on what will happen at the end—to the world, to the Jewish people, and to the individual human being. Topics such as the afterlife, resurrection of the dead, return to Zion, the ingathering of the exiles, the rebuilding of Jerusalem and the Temple are now very much on the agenda of Jewish thinkers. A new contribution to this now fashionable writing is *The Messiah and the Jews* by Rabbi Elaine Rose Glickman, a noted teacher and the award-winning author of *Sacred Parenting: Jewish Wisdom for Your Family's Early Years; Living Torah; B'chol L'vavcha; and Haman and the Jews.*

It takes a great deal of courage to write one book on Jewish beliefs of the Messiah. Jews have been wondering about the character of this individual—how he (or she) will affect our world, and the difference it makes if we do or do not believe in his (or her) imminent arrival. Rabbi Glickman has assembled a treasure house of traditional Jewish teachings of these topics from scripture to the Rabbinic midrash, through medieval philosophers, mysticism, and Hasidism—up to and including a brief chapter on the messianic claims of Chabad's Schneerson—to contemporary liberal Reform Jews. Her major contribution is simply to have researched the topics and succeeded in presenting this rich collection of material,

largely arranged according to topical considerations. A generous
array of footnotes can provide opportunities for further, more
scholarly investigation.

Particularly successful is Rabbi Glickman's treatment of
messianic reflection among classical Reform and modern liberal
Judaism. This is an area that Rabbi Glickman obviously knows very
well from personal experience, which accounts for the serious,
sustained but also relatively modest treatment she accords. She
deserves a great deal of acclaim for bringing her study up to date
with a treatment of both classical and liberal Reform thinking. She
even has the courage to conclude the book with an affirmation of
the Sabbath as itself a messianic statement. This brings the study
to a powerful conclusion.

Though maybe not as comprehensive as a scholarly treatment
may have been—the intention was accessibility for a broad audience,
Jews and non-Jews alike—Rabbi Glickman has presented us with
an immensely useful anthology of Jewish consideration of the
meanings of messianic theology and its relevance to our own lives.
It is not clear, to this writer at least, which of our contemporaries
has a stake in these issues, but if thinking about the end of days
is very much in fashion again, then this book should provide
opportunities for serious study.

—Rabbi Neil Gillman, PhD

PREFACE

"You know what they say about waiting for the messiah, don't you? It doesn't pay much but it's steady work." It's an old Jewish joke and like most such jokes, it contains more than its share of truth. Waiting for the messiah in Judaism is, generally, a fruitless and unrewarding task and it's certainly nothing we bank on having happen anytime soon.

But what we have done, as this volume documents, is turned waiting for the messiah into an art form as well as a vehicle for teaching ethics and spirituality. In other words, it might be a bad thing if the messiah showed up because we've made waiting for the messiah such a potent means of exploring what it means to be a Jew. In this volume, the author provides basic information about the Jewish view of the messiah and how that view developed through the centuries. In addition, she covers topics most readers will probably not have encountered before (e.g., the warrior messiah, Hephzibah) and clarifies the roles played by characters such as Elijah in the messianic narrative. Of course, these topics may be of particular interest to those who are interested in Christianity's definitions of the messiah and his return. Finally, she covers modern messianism (e.g., Rabbi Schneerson) and the response of modern Jewish movements to this ancient concept.

Different Jews, in different eras, had different beliefs about the messiah. For example, some Jews of the Land of Israel (including

Rabbi Akiva) wanted a messiah while others doubted he'd come
to their rescue:

> When Rabbi Akiva saw Bar Kozva, he said: This is the King
> Messiah. Rabbi Yochanan ben Torta said: Akiva! Grass will
> grow in your cheeks and the Messiah will not yet have come!
> (Y. *Taanit* 4:6, PM 24a)

In contrast, in Babylonia, the sages thought of the messiah not
as answer to current problems but as a comforting vision in the
afterlife:

> The Holy One, blessed be He, will make a great banquet
> for the righteous on the day He manifests His love for the
> seed of Isaac. After they have eaten and drunk, the cup of
> Grace will be offered to our father Abraham that he should
> recite Grace, but he will answer them, "I cannot say Grace,
> because Ishmael issued from me." Then Isaac will be asked
> to say Grace, but he will answer them, "I cannot say Grace
> because Esau issued from me." Then Jacob will be asked,
> "Take it and say Grace." But he will reply, "I cannot say
> Grace because I married two sisters during [both] their
> lifetimes whereas the Torah was destined to forbid them
> to me." Then Moses will be asked, "Take it and say Grace."
> He will answer, "I cannot say Grace since I was not privi-
> leged to enter the Land of Israel either in life or in death."
> Then Joshua will be asked, "Take it and say Grace." But he
> will reply, "I cannot say Grace since I was not privileged to
> have a son.".... Then David will be asked, "Take it and say
> Grace." He will reply, "I will say Grace and it is fitting for
> me to say Grace, as it is said, 'I will lift up the cup of salva-
> tion and call upon the name of the Lord.' (Psalm 116:13)"
> (B. *Pesachim* 119b)

Many primary texts are provided which may make this volume useful for those intending to teach a course on Judaism and the messiah. Waiting for the messiah will still be something like waiting to
win the Powerball Lottery: you may hope for it but it is extremely

unlikely that you will win. But reading about the hopes and dreams of those who have shared that experience with you throughout the ages will be a reward unto itself.

—Rabbi Judith Z. Abrams, PhD

INTRODUCTION

I wish that you will make known to me when the Messiah of
the Eternal will come, and what will be after all of this.
—FROM THE APOCALYPSE *SEFER ZERUBBABEL*

I have been waiting for the Messiah since I was fifteen years old.
I didn't realize this right away, of course. At the time I was obsessed equally with a guy in my driver's ed class who did not know my name, how many servings of light ice cream I could eat without exceeding my one-thousand-calorie-a-day limit, and whether I could pull off dramatic eyeliner and dark lipstick (I could not). In my less self-fixated moments I thought about nuclear war, the plight of famine victims, and why some people hit their children.

That was the year I first said to myself: Things have to get better than this.

I thought I was waiting for my driver's license, or a serious boyfriend, or to wake up super-skinny and perfect. I thought I was waiting for disarmament, or hunger relief, or everyone to be kinder.

It wasn't until I got to rabbinical school that I recognized what I was really waiting for.

I was waiting for the Messiah.

You might be waiting for the Messiah, too.

※

We live in a time when optimism might be construed as naiveté, idealism as gullibility. As I write this, the world's economies are in crisis, war and genocide and terrorism fester, and millions go to sleep hungry. Global warming is on the rise, along with hate crimes, joblessness, and the child mortality rate. Schools employ metal detectors and security guards. Nearly half of all marriages end in divorce. An adorable seven-year-old girl I know aspires to be "sexy."

Even among those who appear to be doing fine, depression and anxiety are rampant. There is discontent, unease, gnawing fearfulness that all is not well. Perhaps a seventy-year-old sentiment of Albert Camus puts it most succinctly, and most clearly: "Things as they are, in my opinion, are far from satisfactory.... [People] die, and they are not happy."[1]

That pretty much says it all, doesn't it? And really, who can deny it? Anyone looking clear-eyed at the world around us has to echo Camus: "Things as they are, in my opinion, are far from satisfactory.... [People] die, and they are not happy."

We could probably be forgiven for stopping right there. For accepting "things as they are" and finding glimmers of joy where we can, or despairing entirely, or trying to duck out of this reality and create our own.

But there is something we can do instead. It's the same thing our ancestors have done for thousands of years. It's brave, and defiant, and exhilarating, and crazy in the best possible way.

We can wait for the Messiah.

※

Waiting for the Messiah doesn't mean just sitting around. It doesn't mean writing off the world as it is now. It doesn't mean fomenting religious warfare or throwing off the shackles of socially acceptable behavior. And it doesn't necessarily mean envisioning acts of miraculous deliverance or heavenly rewards for the righteous—although we might be surprisingly moved by accounts of

Now maybe this is just human nature. Suffering is terrible, but suffering for no reason is even worse. If we ascribe some meaning to afflictions—if we see war and disease and cruelty and even the everyday indignities of our own lives as part of a greater design—we might find them explainable, understandable, bearable; we create nobility from degradation, purpose from indifference. And maybe our ancestors were just kidding themselves; after all, millions have been crushed by these footprints of the Messiah—and the Messiah has yet to appear.

Or maybe it is more than that. Maybe Ezekiel was right, and Isaiah was right, and Maimonides was right, and maybe so many generations who have come before us were right as well. Maybe we are right when we dare to believe that there is nobility and purpose in our history, an end and an import to all we've achieved and endured. Maybe we are right when we dare to believe that God is watching, and God cares, and God has a plan—a plan that leaves us dumbstruck and uncomprehending, but a plan nevertheless. Maybe we are right when we look backward in horror, and around us in anguish, and forward in expectation. "Even with all this, I will await his coming every day."

I will. I am an otherwise rational human being, a rabbi, a writer, a wife, a mother. I love people who have died painfully, and too soon. I sometimes cry when I see the news. I know that suffering is real. I know that I am responsible for trying to alleviate as much of that suffering as I can. And I know that no matter how much I do, people will still die, and they will not be happy. I know that things will still be far from satisfactory.

And still I know this: "I believe with perfect faith in the coming of the Messiah, although he may tarry; even with all this, I will await his coming every day."

Maybe you are waiting, too.

❖

What specifically does it mean to wait for the Messiah?

It depends whom we ask. For some, the coming of the Messiah means a restoration of ancient Israel: all Jews will return to the Land, where we will rebuild the Temple, reconsecrate the high priest, and reestablish the system of sacrificial worship. For others, the coming of the Messiah means a universal perfection of humanity by humanity: we will discover and be true to the best within ourselves, and in doing so we will redeem our own world. For some, the coming of the Messiah means a time of warfare and fear: bloody battles will rage, enemies will besiege our cities, and we will triumph only when all seems lost. For others, the coming of the Messiah means a totally altered universe: lions will eat straw and not meat,[3] we will drink thirty kegs of wine from a single grape,[4] the dead will revive.

We may not respond to all of these messianic visions. That's fine; our ancestors didn't either. The Talmud records fiery disagreements about the nature of the Messiah and the timing of his arrival; Maimonides had no patience with the Messiah as described by Jewish apocalypses; and mystics conceived a Messiah impenetrable to all but the initiated. We who love our Diaspora[5] homes might not welcome the idea of living in Israel; we who value prayer and spirituality might be less than delighted with the prospect of worshipping God through animal sacrifice; we who seek peace might not thrill to the image of messianic wars; and we who pride ourselves on logic and intellect might not know quite what to do with a vegetarian lion or an insanely overactive grape.

But in order to discover what we await, we need to learn about and grapple with what our ancestors awaited as well. Their messianic visions reflect the words of the prophets, the narratives of the Bible, the experience of the Jewish people across the generations. Their messianic hopes embody the creativity, the resilience, the insight, and the faith of a singular people with a singular history—and a singular destiny. Let us look at their words with open minds and open hearts; for as we acquaint ourselves with who the Messiah traditionally is and what the Messianic Age traditionally means, we may find our souls stirring, in wakefulness, in recognition, in hope, and maybe even in belief.

For maybe—even with all this—we believe in the Messiah. Maybe we await his coming every day.

CHAPTER ONE

The Messiah Is Coming!

"The Messiah is coming!"

The phrase might conjure images that make us wince: unwashed would-be prophets waving signs outside an office building, bumper stickers warning nonbelievers of earthly misery when the faithful are swept up to heaven, irrational and exuberant and just plain inappropriate proclamations when normal people are simply trying to make it through the day.

It is no wonder we hesitate to say, "The Messiah is coming"—and no wonder we shrink from those who do. It is no wonder—but it is a terrible shame.

For saying, "The Messiah is coming," is not the exclusive province of the fundamentalists, or the evangelicals, or the slightly unhinged. Saying—and believing—that the Messiah is coming is actually a universal privilege—and our special birthright as Jews.

"The Messiah is coming." "Our lives, our history, hold significance and purpose." "God cares for us, and watches over us, and has a plan for us." "What happens to us matters." "Things will get better than this." However we choose to say it, we can—and we should—say it. Saying it has sustained our ancestors for thousands of years, and saying it will sustain us and our children. And letting ourselves believe it—well, that's even better.

The conviction that the Messiah is coming is Judaism's greatest gift to the world. It is a promise of meaning. It is a source of consolation. It is a wellspring of creativity. It is a reconciliation between what is and what should be. And it is perhaps our most powerful statement of faith—in God, in humanity, and in ourselves.

For now, let us understand the words literally or metaphorically, at face value or as an elaborate allegory. But let us begin to say—and even to believe—them:

"The Messiah is coming!"

Where Is the Messiah Now?

If the Messiah is coming but is not yet here, well, then, where is he?

Every generation of Jews calls out these words, and while the question might appear rhetorical, our ancestors actually crafted very specific responses! To some, the Messiah has not yet been born; he will enter the world just like any other infant and live unrecognized until he begins to distinguish himself with mighty acts. For others, the Messiah has actually been here for millennia—in the form of the Jewish community or even all of humanity; according to this view, the Messianic Age will commence as soon as we turn away from cruelty and hatred and fully embrace our capacity for justice, righteousness, and peace.

While we can find wisdom and inspiration in each of these teachings, a different—and much more daring—idea also emerges in messianic tradition: *The Messiah already exists and waits for us, just as we wait for him.*

Not only has God promised the Messiah, then, but God has already brought him into being. Some texts testify that he has been at God's side since—or even during—the time of Creation: "You find that at the beginning of the creation of the world King Messiah was born," the midrash[1] tells, "and that he emerged in the thought [of God] before the world was created."[2] And according to our mystics, the sacred soul of Adam—the first man, whose spirit was formed by the very breath of God (Genesis

2:7) would be embodied again in the Messiah: "The secret of the name Adam ... points to a well-known acronym: Adam, David, [Messiah]," modern scholar Moshe Idel explains. "This acronym means that Adam's soul has been reincarnated in the body of [King] David, who will return as the Messiah.... The Messiah, therefore, will possess the soul that first inhabited Adam and then [King] David."[3]

Another, equally evocative tradition links the Messiah's origin not to the awesome days of Creation, but to one of the darkest periods in Jewish history. In the year 586 BCE, on the ninth day of the Hebrew month of Av, the Babylonians conquered the city of Jerusalem, brutalizing her inhabitants, exiling her people, and razing the Holy Temple. The date—known as Tisha b'Av, literally "the ninth of Av"—has been marked for centuries with fasting, mourning, and lamentation. Yet for some messianists, this same date came to stand as the birthday of the Messiah:

> On the day on which the Temple was destroyed, Elijah of blessed memory[4] was walking along the road. He heard a heavenly voice cry out and say, "The Holy Temple has become a ruin, the children of the Sovereign have gone into captivity!" As soon as Elijah heard this, he said to himself, "Is it God's will to destroy the world?" ... Then a heavenly voice was heard and said, "Let them be, for already their savior has been born."[5]

The concept of an already existing Messiah is intriguing enough, but these traditions also comfort and inspire us. Associating the Messiah with Creation, our ancestors asserted that redemption has been an essential part of God's plan from the very beginning; even before declaring "Let there be light!" (Genesis 1:3), God had already planned for the ultimate salvation of the Jewish people. The connection between the Babylonians' devastating defeat of Jerusalem and the birth of the Messiah proves similarly significant; even in the midst of Israel's greatest suffering, God was preparing the instrument of our deliverance. Neither the existence of the

Messiah nor the trials that induce our longing for him are random; everything is part of a divine order that will culminate in our preordained messianic redemption.

Until that day arrives, however, the Messiah remains hidden. Many sages envision this concealment as pure misery: he is imprisoned and mocked,[6] trapped in a hostile land,[7] suffering in each generation according to its sins,[8] or sobbing in the prophet Elijah's lap as he waits to redeem Israel.[9] The Zohar's magnificent tale "The Bird's Nest" relates that upon seeing the destroyed Temple, "the Messiah lifts up his voice and weeps, and ... the firmament ... shakes, and the fifteen hundred myriads of heavenly angels [tremble], until [his voice] reaches the heavenly throne."[10] The mutuality of our relationship is compelling and heartbreaking: as those he would redeem yearn for him, so does the Messiah long for us.

But not all accounts are so dark. One midrash portrays the Messiah as advocating for Israel in heaven, watching for and immortalizing our acts of righteousness:

> Rabbi Cohen and Rabbi Joshua of Siknin said in the name of Rabbi Levi: ... When a person performs a good deed, who records it? Elijah records it, and the Messiah and the Holy One, blessed be God, subscribe their seal to it.[11]

While he waits for the appointed time of his arrival, then, the Messiah serves as our ally, testifying to our capacity for kindness and compassion. For only by the good deeds he seals can humanity, our ancestors taught, truly prove ourselves worthy of the Messiah.

When Will the Messiah Come?

When will the Messiah come? This question is among the most ancient and stirring of speculations. Our ancestors first gave voice to it nearly three thousand years ago, after the enemy Assyria conquered the northern kingdom of Israel, and their query grew more impassioned with each trial the Jewish people endured. And even in times of tranquility, we have continued to ask; perhaps we are painfully aware that more turmoil may lie just ahead, or perhaps we identify with those who suffer today as our ancestors once did, or perhaps we simply ache for a world better than the one in which we find ourselves.

But for some messianists, the question "When will the Messiah come?" became not only an abstract longing but a concrete challenge. Motivated by a strange brew of theological fervor, existential hunger, and intellectual curiosity, these Jews delved into the ostensibly secret meanings of biblical[12] passages, studied the chronologies recorded in the book of Daniel, conjured the *gematria*—the numerical value—of key words in scripture, and linked historical or current events with messianic literature's enigmatic references to signs that redemption was at hand. The resulting calculations—complex, often convoluted, and occasionally beguiling—purported to reveal the exact time of the Messiah's arrival.

Some of these speculations hewed closely to Jewish teaching. The Messiah would not come on Shabbat, our sages explained, lest Jews seeking to welcome him be forced to violate the Sabbath.[13] Perhaps, some suggested, he would arrive on the eve of Passover, bringing our final redemption on the anniversary of our first redemption.[14] Or, others advised, he might come in the Hebrew month of Tishrei—the first month of the Jewish year and the anniversary of Creation.[15]

But other reckonings, attempting a more definite answer, strained tradition—and credulity. Many of the outstanding sages cited in the Talmud[16] claimed to know exactly when the Messiah would come, but they frequently disagreed with one another, and history would prove them all incorrect. Medievalists posited 1096 CE as the advent of the Messiah and were crushed when the year brought not deliverance but devastation at the hands of the Christian Crusaders. The *Zohar* records several mutually exclusive dates for redemption, and the great scholar and poet Judah HaLevi unapologetically based his messianic calculations upon an especially vivid dream.[17] Dramatic events in the non-Jewish world—from the rise of Islam to the voyage of Columbus—also sparked strong, but no less reliable convictions about when the Messiah would be revealed.

For all of their fallibility, however, these speculations influenced our ancestors tremendously and at times led to behavior that was not in their best interest. Our ancient Rabbis' belief that the Messiah would come soon after Jerusalem's fall to Rome in 70 CE likely helped inspire the catastrophic Bar Kochba Revolt, which took place only sixty-five years later. In 1211, goaded by promises of the Messiah's imminent arrival, France and England's most eminent Jews set out for Jerusalem;[18] and some scholars hold messianic calculations in large part responsible for the disastrous rise of Shabbatei Zevi, a seventeenth-century false messiah whose pretensions inflamed—and then left despondent—much of the Jewish world. On a smaller scale, failed messianic speculations led to misery, depression, and a lack of faith; a Crusader likely gave voice to his Jewish victims' own fears when he mocked them, "Ye have calculated the times of Redemption and they are now past, and the hope of salvation is over and gone."[19]

It was, then, perhaps no wonder that Jewish leaders discouraged calculating the time of redemption.[20] The Talmud offers this delightful analysis: "Three things come unawares: the Messiah, a found article, and a scorpion."[21] and Rabbi Yochanan ben Zakkai's famous admonition not to interrupt planting trees in order to greet the Messiah[22] is often interpreted as skepticism toward those who might unreliably herald the arrival of Israel's savior. Even the sage Rabbi Jose, who engaged in such speculation before the Bar Kochba Revolt, was sufficiently chastened afterward to declare that "one who attempts to give [a date] to the End [of Days] has no share in the World to Come."[23] Early German mystics warned, "If you see one making prophecies about the Messiah, you should know that he deals deeds of witchcraft ... and at the end he will be shamed and despised by the world ... for no one knows anything about the coming of the Messiah."[24] And no less an authority than Moses Maimonides taught, "Neither should one calculate the End. The sages said, 'May the spirit of those who calculate the End be blown away.' But let him wait and believe in the matter generally, as we have explained."[25]

Yet it was also perhaps no wonder that despite the challenge and the hardship, the warnings and the almost-certain possibility of heartache, messianic speculation has continued in virtually every generation.[26] Our yearning is great, our patience sorely tried, and our desire to apprehend something, anything, of God's plan outweighs all the reasons we should know better. Calculating the end may prove irresistibly compelling—as it did, in fact, for Maimonides. The towering figure of Jewish law and philosophy once wrote a letter explicitly forbidding messianic speculation. Ironically, it ended with these words:

> There exists among us a great and wonderful tradition which I received from my father, and he in turn from his father, and his grandfather, who likewise received it, and so through a continuous chain to the beginning of the exile from Jerusalem.... The sign heralding the coming of the Messiah will therefore transpire in the year 4976, i.e. 1216 CE.[27]

Can We Make the Messiah Come Faster?

As if predicting the advent of the Messiah were not compelling enough, our ancestors posed an even more intoxicating possibility: we could actually hasten his arrival.

That the Messiah would come was a given. But for some, the time of his appearance was predestined, woven into the fabric of the universe since Creation, unyielding and inevitable. We could ponder it, perhaps even calculate it—but we could not alter it. But for others, God had put into our hands the date of redemption. If we undertook just the right action, we ourselves could usher in the Messianic Age.

What was this right action? Most messianists—from Talmudic sages to mystical teachers to modern liberals—linked the Messianic Age to religious and ethical living.[28] The Talmud illustrates this concept in a beautiful and poignant passage:

Rabbi Joshua ben Levi encounters Elijah the prophet and asks him, "When will the Messiah come?" "Go and ask him yourself," Elijah replies. "He is sitting at the entrance to the city of Rome, among the poor and the diseased. They unwind all of their bandages at once, then rewind them; but he unwinds and rewinds the bandages one at a time, so that if he is summoned there shall be no delay in his arrival." After finding and greeting the man destined to be the Messiah, Rabbi Joshua asks when he will reveal himself as Israel's Redeemer. "Today," the Messiah replies. But the day passes, and Rabbi Joshua complains to Elijah, "The Messiah lied to me, for he said, 'Today I shall come,' and he did not come." But Elijah has an explanation: "This is what he told you," Elijah corrects Rabbi Joshua. "Today—if you hearken to God's voice."[29]

If the Jewish people hearken to God's voice—that is, unite to do God's will—we can induce the Messiah to arrive. But hearkening to God's voice is, of course, not so easy. Mysticism—including much of Hasidism and Kabbalah[30]—defined it as no less than the perfection of our souls; only by redeeming the divine potential within each of us would we merit a redeemed universe. Early Reform Judaism charged us with actually redeeming the universe ourselves; if we worked tirelessly enough for social justice, expended sufficient effort on behalf of those who lacked, and recognized in each human face the image of God, we could transform the world and achieve our own salvation. And Azariah Figo, a renowned seventeenth-century preacher in Venice, taught:

> The purpose of the exile [is] to teach us humility and discipline. We do not seem to feel the exile.... Our houses are filled with all good things; we and our sons and daughters dress in silks and ornaments like the nobility, and we bring to our table royal delicacies like [King] Solomon in all his pomp, just like the time of our prosperity when we lacked nothing.... *For the postponement of the [End of Days] we ourselves are responsible.*[31]

Although these demands—perfected souls, universal justice, sorrowful asceticism—might appear impossibly onerous, far less daunting prescriptions proved equally out of reach. The *Zohar* states that if one community atones sincerely, the Messiah will come;[32] the Talmud envisions requirements as simple as keeping two Sabbaths in a row[33] or a single day of repentance.[34] Even with such minimal requirements, however, we have yet to behold our deliverer—demonstrating, according to tradition, not a failure on the part of God or the Messiah but a failure of the Jewish people to meet our most basic obligations. Perhaps for this reason our ancestors sought comfort in the teaching of ancient sage Rabbi Joshua ben Levi: "If we are worthy, God will speed [the arrival of the Messiah]. If not, he will come at the appointed time."[35] While right action would indeed hasten our redemption, our shortcomings would not prevent it.

And if history is any indication, we will have to wait for "the appointed time." After all, the likelihood of every single Jew banding together to observe Shabbat (twice in a row, no less!) or engage in complete repentance—let alone perfect ourselves, bring justice to every corner of the world, or renounce fine food and clothing—is virtually nil. Yet we still find meaning in the idea that our behavior can summon the Messiah. On a practical level, of course, it encourages religious and moral values, offering a possible—only remotely possible, but still possible—reward for living as God commands us; but this teaching's spiritual underpinnings are even more significant.

God cares. God watches what we do, and God responds. God expects great things from us—things like saving the world—but God is willing to settle for less—for even one day of atonement. And God wants to redeem us—so much so that if we work together to achieve just an iota of the goodness of which we are capable, God will instantly alter a divine plan that has existed since the days of Creation and speed the Messiah's arrival. If only we want it enough, messianic tradition teaches, the Messiah can come. The Messiah can even come "today—if [we] hearken to God's voice."

How Will the Messiah Appear?

While pondering the *when* of the Messiah's arrival captivated our ancestors, envisioning the *how* proved almost as fascinating. Accounts of our redeemer's first appearance offer wonderful glimpses into the Jewish imagination, as well as deeply held beliefs about the nature of our people and the import of our salvation.

For some, deliverance would unfold gradually—so slowly, in fact, that we would not even be aware of its beginnings. A beautiful midrash relates:

> It is told of Rabbi Hiyya and Rabbi Simeon that they walked in the valley of Arbela early in the morning and saw the dawn breaking on the horizon. Thereupon Rabbi Hiyya said, "So too is Israel's redemption; at first it will be only very slightly visible, then it will shine forth more brightly, and only afterwards will it break forth in all of its glory."[36]

This theme found its echo among many would-be calculators of the Messiah, who painstakingly divided the Messianic Age into stages—from the return of all Jews to Israel to the resurrection of the dead—and sought to determine when each would commence and for how long it would last. Also affirming Rabbi Hiyya's teaching were post-Emancipation Jews who believed that humanity—slowly realizing our potential for good and our obligation to heal the world—would enact a progressive but certain redemption.

Others, however, anticipated a distinctly messianic figure. With images that reflected both their expectation of glory and their experience of degradation, our ancestors predicted in often elaborate detail the advent of our redeemer. And because no single account became authoritative, messianic literature retained—and regarded—two compelling, but altogether contradictory, depictions of the Messiah's appearance.

The first portrait develops as we might expect: a scene of splendor, a magnificent icon at its center. Some rabbis called the Messiah *Bar Nifle* or *Anani*—phrases translated as "Son [or He] of the Clouds"[37]—amplifying a biblical prophecy that our savior would reveal himself from on high. One early text recounts: "I dreamed a dream by night; and I beheld, and lo! There arose a violent wind from the sea ... and the wind caused the likeness of a form of a man to come out of the heart of the seas. And this Man flew with the clouds of heaven."[38] "And now let us speak in praise of King Messiah," another passage rejoices, "who will come in the future with the clouds of heaven and two *Seraphim* [fiery angels] to his right and to his left, as it is written: 'Behold, with the clouds of heaven come one like unto a son of man.'"[39]

Despite its seemingly irresistible appeal, however, the image of a Messiah descending from the skies holds only limited influence. Perhaps our ancestors were unnerved by its similarity to biblical accounts of God riding upon clouds[40] and sought to clarify that not even the acclaimed Messiah approached the glory of the Divine. Indeed, other, equally exultant sources take pains to praise our redeemer in strictly earthly terms, personifying him as "a white bull with large horns"[41] or a lion—the symbol of the tribe of Judah, from whom the Messiah will be descended.

Yet something even more significant prevented our ancestors from embracing a savior of such otherworldly grandeur. In a passage traditionally associated with the advent of the Messiah, the biblical prophet Zechariah heralds a king "triumphant yet humble—riding on a donkey, on a donkey foaled by a she-ass" (Zechariah 9:9).[42] And the most stirring descriptions of the Messiah's arrival are not those that exalt his majesty, but those that explore his weakness.

After all, what makes the tale of Rabbi Joshua ben Levi—he of the dashed expectations that the Messiah would appear "today"—so striking and so tragic is that it functions on two levels: while we who await the Messiah suffer, so does the Messiah suffer himself. Here the Messiah does not pass grandly through clouds or tame the currents of ocean winds; rather, he sits unnoticed among the outcast and the ill, unwinding and rewinding bandages, tending anonymously to bloody wounds.

And it is this figure that prevails in messianic tradition. Among the names by which the Messiah will be known, the Talmud relates, is "the Leprous of the House of Study."[43] And Hasidic literature spins wrenching tales of would-be Messiahs forced to live as lepers and beggars because the world was not yet ready for redemption. According to one story, the Ba'al Shem Tov[44] and a disciple visited a destitute home:

> And, behold, in the ruined house lived an old man, a leper; from head to foot there was no hale spot in his body, he was so full of wounds and boils.... And when the Ba'al Shem opened the door, the old man became filled with joy, and ran up to the Ba'al Shem ... and [one] who saw not their joy has never seen joy in [one's] life.... And [when] they took [leave] from each other, [they] parted from each other in fierce love.

When the disciple asks why the leper and the Ba'al Shem Tov were so delighted with one another, the Hasidic master replies:

> There is a Messiah in every generation in this world, in reality, clothed in a body. And if the generation is worthy, he is ready to reveal himself; and if, God forbid, they are not worthy, he departs. And behold, that old man was ready to be our True Messiah.[45]

In a similar narrative, a poor beggar enters a town seeking Shabbat hospitality; but cruel boys and an arrogant rabbi refuse him. When the citizens realize the beggar is really the Messiah, they rush to offer a proper welcome; but they "found him not," the fable concludes mournfully, "for a pillar of fire had come and taken him from there."[46]

Why did these miserable figures endure, and why do they move us more than the descriptions of an awesome redeemer? Perhaps it is because the image of a debased Messiah rang true and beautiful to our ancestors, and rings true to us; perhaps we see in him our history—and ourselves.

For our Jewish story is not of import because we began glorious and remained glorious. We began not as nobles but as strangers and slaves—wandering, oppressed, and despised—and from these sad origins would arise as a nation of priests and a holy people. Surely, then, we identify with a Messiah who hides among the lepers, who begs in the villages, who endures and hurts and waits to reveal his greatness. Surely only this one who lives our anguish can achieve our redemption. And in his transformation from sufferer to savior, surely the Messiah would come to embody the journey—and the purpose—of our people.

Has the Messiah Been Revealed Before?

The short answer to this question is "no." The longer answer is "no, but."

When this question is posed, of course, the inquirer is most often asking whether Judaism views Jesus as the Messiah. In this case, we may respond with our short answer: "No." A belief that Jesus was the Messiah is what most separates Jewish from Christian faith, and the Jewish and Christian concepts of redemption. Jesus did not possess the lineage traditionally required of the Messiah,[47] nor—more importantly—did he fulfill the tasks assigned to our redeemer.[48] Throughout the ages Jews have viewed Jesus as everything from a gifted teacher to a dangerous blasphemer, but we have not called him the Messiah. Those who call him Messiah can no longer be accepted as committed Jews, no matter how passionately they claim to be. They are professing Christianity.

But Jesus has not been the only ostensible Messiah to arise among the Jewish people. In countless generations, from ancient times to our own, would-be saviors have proclaimed themselves or allowed enthusiastic followers to proclaim them. These men often possessed remarkable personal magnetism, offered hope during or just after an especially traumatic period, or appeared to fulfill the predictions of messianic calculators. Although none of these messiahs proved legitimate, many attracted fervent adherents and enjoyed tremendous power in the Jewish community, and their unmasking as mere pretenders often brought devastating consequences, from failed military campaigns to mass conversions among disillusioned believers.[49]

Less than two centuries after the birth of Jesus—and less than seventy years after the destruction of the Second Temple—Jews living under Roman occupation encountered another messianic figure: the charismatic and ruthless military leader Bar Kochba. His very name reflected the expectations of his followers; *Bar Kochba*, which literally means "son of a star," alludes to a biblical prophecy that a "star" will rise from Jacob to vanquish the enemies of Israel (Numbers 24:17). Widely celebrated as Israel's redeemer—even the renowned Rabbi Akiva stood among his supporters—Bar Kochba amassed an army to lead an apocalyptic battle against Rome. Although he managed to recapture Jerusalem, the campaign lasted only three years and finally collapsed in the hill country of Bethar. After defeating Bar Kochba, the Romans unleashed their wrath and vengeance upon the Jews, persecuting, massacring, and enslaving survivors. What had begun as the supposed final battle for Israel ended not in triumph but in further humiliation and misery for the Jewish nation.

While the impact of Bar Kochba was unique in its scope and aftermath, he would not be the only false messiah to lead Israel astray. Some followers of the fifth-century Moses of Crete—a handsome preacher who announced himself as Israel's redeemer—converted in despair to Christianity once his pretensions were revealed. In the ninth century, Yehuda Yudghan claimed to be the forerunner of the Messiah but led his adherents to conversion to Islam. During the sixteenth century, inflamed by the messianic aspirations of a Jew named David Reuveni, Diego Pires—the child of Marranos, Jews who had converted to Christianity under pressure from the Spanish monarchy during the Inquisition—abandoned his prestigious government post, renamed himself Shlomo Molcho, and traveled to Rome, where he was warmly greeted as the Messiah. Fearful of the effect Molcho might have on Catholic authority, already rendered unstable by the Reformation, the

Inquisitors burned him at the stake. His inspiration, David Reuveni, was imprisoned and died in a dungeon cell.

But the messianic pretender par excellence is the seventeenth-century Shabbatei Zevi, who, aided by his so-called prophet Nathan, convinced Jews from virtually every region of the world that he was the true Messiah. After enduring the Inquisition, the expulsion from Spain, and the Chmielnicki Massacre in Eastern Europe—as well as immersing themselves in the doctrines of Lurianic Kabbalah, which suggested an imminent redemption—his people hungered for salvation, and Shabbatei Zevi obliged by announcing himself as the Messiah in 1648 in Smyrna.[50] The reception he enjoyed was unprecedented: conventional calendar dating was replaced with references to "the first year of the renewal of the prophecy and the kingdom";[51] Jews sold all they owned in preparation for a new life in Israel; prayer books featured images of Shabbatei and King David, the traditional ancestor of the Messiah;[52] and enterprising Jews offered odds on how many years would pass before Shabbatei was formally anointed as sovereign over Jerusalem. Shabbatei's widespread acceptance is all the more striking in that he preached undeniably heretical practices, publicly pronouncing the Tetragrammaton, the Holy and Ineffable Name of God, traditionally uttered only by the high priest on Yom Kippur when the Temple still stood in Jerusalem; composing a blessing that praised God as the One who "allows the forbidden";[53] ordering fasts and acts of self-abnegation; and exalting his most loyal believers as messianic kings.

Alarmed by Shabbatei's influence, which was beginning to spread into the gentile community, Turkish authorities arrested the would-be redeemer in 1666. Shabbatei continued to captivate followers even from his cell, however, and finally his jailers forced him to choose between converting to Islam and being put to death. His adoption of Islam stunned his flock, many of whom either refused to accept the news or attempted to rationalize his apostasy as a necessary messianic act. After his conversion—and even after his death in 1676—Shabbatei Zevi and the movement he inspired retained a strong hold on a not insignificant segment of the Jewish people.[54]

These stories of false redeemers may appear ridiculous or far-fetched. We may shake our heads and wonder how our ancestors could have been so silly, so easily manipulated, so played for fools. But neither is our time immune to the lure of messianic pretenders. Scholar Edward Gewirtz intriguingly argues that nationalism, socialism, and scientism are false messiahs, movements that promise a salvation they cannot deliver.[55] Some see a similar phenomenon in Hasidic Lubavitchers' devotion to their Rebbe, Menachem Mendel Schneerson, and the expectation of some that he will soon be resurrected to continue his leadership.[56]

Who is to say that we will not fall prey to a false messiah as easily as our ancestors did if we face trials that can be borne only by anticipating redemption or if someone arises who pledges eternal peace in return for our loyalty? And if such a person does arise, how will we know if he is telling the truth?

How Can We Recognize the True Messiah?

It might appear impossible to know when the Messiah has truly arrived. Myriad descriptions of the Messiah reflect myriad worldviews, myriad historical events, myriad theological and philosophical understandings. One tradition asserts that the Messiah waits for us in heaven; another explains that he simply has yet to be born. The Messiah will ride upon the clouds, some sources promise; others predict he will emerge from a crowd of beggars. Depending on which texts we consult, we find that the Messiah will be a special person, or an otherworldly figure, or perhaps an entire community.

In the face of so many ideas, how are we to say what makes a messiah legitimate? How are we to know when our savior has come?

We will know, Judaism counsels, as long as we seek redemption rather than a redeemer. After all, anyone can claim to be our redeemer, and many have. *But not even the most successful messianic pretenders were able to achieve redemption.*

It is so simple, and yet so clear and true: we will recognize the Messiah not because of the way he looks, not because of a forceful personality or esoteric origin, but because he will accomplish the messianic tasks. *We will recognize the Messiah because he will bring redemption.*

As we will see, messianic redemption means different things to different people. For Moses Maimonides and the philosophers, it was the opportunity to live free and safe, focusing our energies on achieving deepest knowledge of God. For our Talmudic sages, it was the fulfillment of the exalted oracles of our biblical prophets and the revival of the Temple in Jerusalem. For medieval apocalyptics, it was the cosmic triumph of Israel over enemies who sought her destruction. And for some mystics as well as early Reform Jews, it was the perfection of our world—and our souls—by humanity itself.

While each of these messianic hopes may appear unique, they are all clearly united in theme: The Messiah will change the world for the better. The Messiah will guide us to work for—even to fight for—what is right. The Messiah will nurture the divine spark within each of us and bring us closer to understanding God and what God requires of us. The Messiah will deliver us into a time of prosperity, justice, and peace. The Messiah will redeem us from the evil in this universe and in ourselves.

In the next chapters, we will examine more specific—and sometimes more challenging and more baffling—traditions about what the Messiah will accomplish and what will constitute messianic redemption. Some of these teachings will speak to us and inspire us. Others will bewilder us or repel us. Yet we will recognize in even the most difficult, most inaccessible passages our conviction that life, and history, have meaning and purpose. We will recognize our conviction that a divine plan exists for the universe. We will recognize our conviction that things have to get better than this.

And sadly, we will recognize that redemption—and our redeemer—still tarry. For looking at our world as it is today, we are tragically aware of all the messianic tasks yet to be completed; we are tragically certain that the Messiah has yet to be revealed. In the haunting words of Elie Wiesel:

> *If I told you that I believe in God, I would be lying.*
> *If I told you that I did not believe in God, I would be lying.*
> *If I told you that I believe in man, I would be lying.*
> *If I told you I did not believe in man, I would be lying.*
> *But one thing I do know: the Messiah has not come yet.*[57]

CHAPTER TWO

The Messiah Will Rule Over Israel

There is a beautiful Israeli folk song whose lyrics contain these words:

> *From above the peak of Mount Scopus, peace upon*
> *you, Jerusalem!*
> *Thousands of exiles from the ends of the earth lift*
> *their eyes up to you.*
> *With thousands of blessings be blessed, holy place of*
> *kings, city of royalty.*
> *Jerusalem! Jerusalem! I will not budge from this*
> *place!*
> *Jerusalem! Jerusalem! The Messiah will come, he will*
> *come!*[1]

For nearly three thousand years the Messiah has been linked with our Holy Land, our Zion, our Israel. The Messiah's forebear King David united and ruled over the Land, establishing Jerusalem as the eternal capital of the Jewish people, and according to traditional messianic expectations, a return of all Jews to sovereign Israel will inaugurate the reign of the Messiah. For our ancestors, the Messiah and Israel were virtually inseparable: one could not exist without the other.

It's incredible, isn't it? After thousands of years of exile, Israel continued to tug at our hearts and our souls; this strip of land remained sacred even to those who had built successful lives in the Diaspora, even to those who could have made aliyah[2] but chose not to. And although we might expect Moses, our most celebrated redeemer, to capture the messianic imagination, he pales before David, Israel's most celebrated king.

Why this unique relationship between Israel and the Messiah, between our land and our redemption? And how to resolve the complexities that arose from this connection in ancient times and in ours? What happens if we desperately want the Messiah to come but Israel languishes in the grip of non-Jewish rulers? And what if Israel stands firmly in Jewish hands but the Messiah has not yet arrived?

Let us continue.

What Does "Messiah" Mean?

"Messiah" comes from the Hebrew word *mashiach*, whose root, *mem-shin-chet* (*m-sh-ch*), means "to anoint"; thus *mashiach* refers to someone who has been anointed. That definition, of course, raises new and more complex questions: What does it mean to be anointed? And who has been anointed before?

Despite the grand and majestic visions the word "anointed" might conjure, the act it describes is actually pretty simple: oil is poured onto a person's head. Anointing is not unique to Judaism; archaeological evidence demonstrates, in fact, that the rite of anointing kings originated in Egypt and was practiced by the Canaanites even before the Israelites entered the Promised Land.[3]

Still, anointing took on a special role in Jewish tradition. Priests and recovered lepers were anointed, and once Israel began crowning kings of her own, anointing became an essential feature of their coronation.[4] The anointing of kings likely took place on Rosh Hashanah[5] and over time came to be accompanied by joyful processions, feasts, special sacrifices, and the sounding of the sho-far.[6] The oil used to anoint King Solomon was stored in the *aron*, the holy ark, further suggesting a sacred aspect to the ceremony (1 Kings 1:39).

The relationship between being anointed (the verb form of *m-sh-ch*) and being called an anointed one (the noun form of *m-sh-ch*) is complicated, however. According to the Bible, *merely experiencing anointment is not enough to earn the specific title of messiah—anointed one (mashiach)*. In fact, of all the priests, lepers, and rulers anointed in the Bible, only three are named and designated anointed ones—that is, messiahs.[7]

All three of them are kings.[8] The first monarch over Israel, King Saul, is also the first to be known as an anointed one—as messiah. As we might assume, the Bible next calls King David—the second and most illustrious sovereign over Israel—messiah and, as we probably would not assume, even extends this title to a non-Jewish ruler, Cyrus, king of Persia.

Now what is going on here? If Jewish tradition holds that the Messiah has not yet appeared, how can the Bible be pronouncing people messiahs—and three of them, no less?

Let us explore further the definition—and the significance—of the term "messiah" in biblical times. You may have noticed that when I refer to the Bible's characterization of Saul, David, and Cyrus as messiahs, I use a lowercase *m*. I've done this to underscore the fact that *the Bible uses the word "messiah" not as a proper name for a single ultimate redeemer, but primarily as a description*. In the biblical context, the noun form of "messiah" denotes an ordinary person singled out—that is, literally and symbolically anointed—by God to advance the cause of Israel.

And the achievements of these three men, while remarkable, are not of the cosmic or supernatural variety; they are limited strictly to the military and political realms. As the first sovereign over Israel, Saul united the tribes, defeated the enemy Ammonites and Amalekites, and drove the Philistines out of Judah. David completely subdued the Philistines, extended his kingdom's border all the way to the Euphrates River, overthrew Israel's foes Moab and Edom, made treaties with the influential nations Geshur and

Phoenicia, and of course brought Jerusalem into Jewish hands for the first time. While he himself was not Jewish, Cyrus became a hero to the Jews exiled by the Babylonians; when his people, the Persians, conquered Babylon, Cyrus explicitly permitted the Jews to return to the Land of Israel and rebuild the Temple.[9]

Although the Messiah we will examine in the rest of this book is very different from these three men, still he bears their influence. His character and his tasks reflect the achievements of these early messiahs, especially those of King David, but perhaps his most essential element is being anointed, being selected, by God. According to the Bible, Saul, David, and Cyrus achieved their purposes because they were meant to do so, because God wanted them to do so. God had anointed them—that is, God had brought them to power—and they in turn fulfilled part of God's plan. They were, therefore, the first messiahs. While the scope of the capital-M Messiah will be so much greater, he too will be distinguished less by his mighty acts than by the fact that God anointed him to perform them.

Why Must the Messiah Be Descended from King David?

The short answer to this question is "because the Bible says so." But let us look first at the long answer.

King David is a figure unrivaled in Jewish history. His military triumphs, his political savvy, his charisma and strength of personality are unparalleled. Even his relationship with God approached that of Moses; David is credited with composing much of the book of Psalms, and although his son Solomon actually built it, David conceived the glorious Temple in Jerusalem. It was temptingly easy to believe that such a magnificent reign would continue, eternally successful in the hands of King David and his offspring.

And certain historical events did appear to legitimize this view. David's descendant Hezekiah—the only monarch to enjoy a level of regard even approaching that of David—ruled over the southern kingdom of Judah when Assyria conquered the northern kingdom of Israel. For a fearsome and desperate time, it seemed that the Assyrians would overcome Judah as well; then, apparently miraculously, Judah was spared. The episode extended the survival of the Davidic dynasty in Judah and, because it occurred during Hezekiah's reign, reinforced the prophet Isaiah's conviction that God intended to fulfill the messianic promise through Hezekiah.[10] Scholar Joseph Klausner holds that the prophet Jeremiah had a comparable experience with Zedekiah, another Judean king descended from David; Zedekiah's efforts to liberate the Hebrew slaves of Jerusalem, as well as his demeanor and attention to Jeremiah's concerns, early on kindled Jeremiah's hope that Zedekiah would serve as the Messiah.[11]

None of this, of course, came to pass. What followed, rather, made agonizingly clear that the Messiah's arrival had been delayed. The Babylonian Exile devastated the Jewish community, and even after King Cyrus allowed the Jews to return to Israel to rebuild the Temple—now called the Second Temple—life there failed to meet the people's exalted expectations. Over the next centuries, a series of non-Jewish rulers presided over the Land, and while Jewish sovereignty returned under Judah Maccabee and his brothers in 165 BCE, it was surrendered to Rome just a hundred years later.[12] A passionate revolt mounted by the Jews in 66 CE against the detested Roman occupiers failed, with crushing consequences that included the destruction of the Second Temple. In the face of such disasters, nostalgia swelled for a better time—the time of King David—and the sense grew that only his progeny could possibly possess the skills and spirit necessary to oversee Israel's restoration and redemption.

On a more practical level, the belief that the true Messiah would arise from King David helped preserve the status quo of power and influence in postexilic Israel. As verifying someone's tribal ancestry became virtually impossible, no one—including would-be usurpers or messianic pretenders—could convincingly challenge the Jewish elite by claiming to be a descendant of David.

Perhaps aware of this issue, the authors of the Gospels according to Matthew (1:1–17) and Luke (3:23–38) took pains to establish Jesus's Davidic credentials, and in a continuation of the "is he really from King David's line or isn't he?" controversy, modern Jewish scholars point to inconsistencies and impossibilities in these genealogies to bolster their argument that Jesus was not the Messiah.

For messianic tradition is adamant on this issue. Looking at our "short answer" in further depth, we find the Bible stating unequivocally that the Messiah must belong to the House of David. References to the Davidic Messiah pervade the books of the prophets and appear in the psalms, but the most famous—and most stirring—testimony comes from the prophet Isaiah:

> *A shoot shall grow out of the stump of [King David's*
> *   father] Jesse,*
> *A twig shall sprout from his stock.*
> *The spirit of the Eternal shall alight upon him:*
> *A spirit of wisdom and insight,*
> *A spirit of counsel and valor,*
> *A spirit of devotion and reverence for the Eternal....*
> *In that day,*
> *The stock of Jesse that has remained standing*
> *Shall become a standard to peoples—*
> *Nations shall seek his counsel*
> *And his abode shall be honored.* (Isaiah 11:1–2, 11:10)

Isaiah—and biblical tradition—makes it quite clear: the Messiah is to be not only King David's spiritual descendant, echoing his most noble qualities, but his physical descendant as well.

So there are two reasons that the Messiah must be descended from King David: because of the teachings of the Bible, and because of King David's own unique character. David beautifully embodies what Klausner called "redemptive dualism"[13]—the political and the pious aspects of an authentic redeemer—and thus serves as "the true prototype of the Messiah."[14]

Why Do Messianic Hopes Focus on Israel?

It is almost impossible to overstate the significance of the Land of Israel in Jewish tradition. And it is almost impossible to overstate the longing of our ancestors to be restored to this precious land.

We who live in the age of modern Israel may find this depth of emotion difficult to understand. We may take her existence for granted; we may feel fulfilled and happy in the Diaspora; we may be too conflicted by the Palestinian dilemma to embrace Israel wholeheartedly. These reservations, however, are luxuries few of our ancestors enjoyed. They knew all too well what could happen to a people who for two thousand years lacked a homeland, who relied on the less-than-reliable hospitality of Diaspora nations—and they believed that God intended Israel to be the place that would finally and fully end their troubles and finally and fully fulfill their messianic hopes.

Later in this chapter we will examine the relationship between the Messiah and the modern State of Israel. For now, however, let us look at the relationship between the Messiah and the idealized Israel of our ancestors.

There was definitely a practical component to our ancestors' yearning. Without a sovereign homeland—a place to belong unquestioningly—they remained essentially powerless, persecuted or exiled or slaughtered at the whims of often hostile rulers. In no small measure their messianic vision reflected that most human and universal desire: a place to live safe and free. The only place in Jewish history that had ever afforded such an opportunity was Israel; Israel, therefore, became the focus of their hopes and aspirations.

But of course the connection also ran much deeper. The Land of Israel served as the tangible sign of their close relationship with God; according to the midrash, God had told Moses, "The Land is beloved to Me, and Israel is beloved to Me. Therefore will I bring Israel, My beloved people, into the beloved Land."[15] God had promised them Israel, promised they would flourish within its

borders as long as they lived up to the divine covenant. To return
to the Land, then, meant also to be returned to God's favor, to be
returned to the best within themselves. As Moses prophesized in
the wilderness:

> When ... you and your children heed God's command with
> all your heart and soul ... then the Eternal your God will
> restore your fortunes and take you back in love.... Even if
> your dispersed are at the ends of the world, from there the
> Eternal your God will gather you; from there God will fetch
> you. And the Eternal your God shall bring you to the land
> in which your forebears dwelt, and you shall dwell in it.
> (Deuteronomy 30:1–5)

The Land took on an almost mystical significance. By the end of the
Second Temple period, our ancestors were calling Israel *ha'aretz*;
Israel was "*the* land"—so exalted it required no further identification, not even a proper name. And the Torah's[16] teaching that
some ritual *mitzvot*—ritual commandments—could be performed
only in Israel came to be reflected in a wider sense that Israel's
very soil was uniquely special, uniquely blessed. The medieval sage
and poet Judah HaLevi gave voice to this feeling most beautifully
in his "Ode to Zion":

> *I would bow down, my face on your ground,*
> *I would love your stones, your dust would move me*
> *   to pity....*
> *The air of your land is the very life of the soul,*
> *The grains of your dust are flowing myrrh,*
> *Your rivers are honey from the comb....*
> *Happy is the one who waits and lives to see your*
> *   light rising,*
> *Your dawn breaking forth!*
> *That one shall rejoice in your joy.*[17]

Finally, our ancestors' longing for the Land of Israel represented
their longing for everything to be made right. As the sixteenth-century Rabbi Judah Loew ben Bezalel—the same rabbi credited with

fashioning a golem, incidentally—explained, "Exile is an unnatu-ral condition. The natural state is for each people to dwell on its own soil.... The present condition of Israel ... is a break in the order of the universe which must be mended."[18] The restoration of the Jewish people to the Land of Israel would demonstrate the mending of this break and the return of order to the universe; and just as unnatural exile would yield to natural sovereignty, so too would the way things are yield to the way things should be.

For the nearly three-thousand-year-old hope is not simply to return to Israel. Were this so, all the Jews exiled by the Babylonians would have gone back as soon as King Cyrus allowed—but many did not. Were this so, all the Jews in nineteenth-century Europe choosing between citizenship in the Diaspora and emigration to Palestine would have made the journey to Israel—but many did not. Were this so, all the Jews in late-nineteenth-century America would have denounced the document in which Reform rabbis asserted, "We ... expect neither a return to Palestine, nor ... the restoration of any of the laws concerning the Jewish state"[19]—but many did not.

Our ancestors who longed for Israel did so not only because it was such a sacred and singular place to live, but because only in such a sacred and singular place could their messianic hopes be realized.

What Is the "Ingathering of the Exiles"?

Although the term "ingathering of the exiles" may appear unfamil-iar, its corresponding Hebrew, *kibbutz galuyot*, contains a word that is actually very well-known. *Kibbutz*—the same *kibbutz* that refers to communal settlements in Israel—means "to gather," and *kib-butz galuyot*, "the ingathering of the exiles," refers to the belief that every Jew from every corner of the earth will come to dwell in Israel at the beginning of the Messianic Age. So crucial—and so wondrous—is this event that Jews traditionally pray for it three times a day; in the words of the *Amidah*'s[20] tenth benediction: "Sound the great shofar for our freedom, and raise the banner to gather in our exiled people, and gather us together from the four corners of the earth. You are blessed, Eternal One, Gatherer of the dispersed of Your people Israel."

How will all this happen? And what will it signify?

From 722 BCE, the year the northern kingdom of Israel fell to Assyria, our ancestors awaited the ingathering of the exiles. Their hopes, however, were dashed when the Babylonians in 586 BCE overran the southern kingdom of Judah and exiled her people as well. What had been glorious, sovereign Israel now stood bereft, virtually empty of Jews. Such a cataclysm was almost beyond comprehension, and the biblical prophets understood that only God could make it right.

With stirring words Jeremiah consoled and inspired the exiles in Babylon:

> *I will build you firmly again, O Maiden Israel!*
> *Again you shall take up your timbrels and go forth to*
> *the rhythm of the dancers.*
> *Again you shall plant vineyards on the hills of*
> *Samaria....*
> *I will bring them in from the northland, gather them*
> *from the ends of the earth—*
> *The blind and the lame among them, those with child*
> *and those in labor—*
> *In a vast throng they shall return here.*
> *They shall come with weeping, and with compassion*
> *I will guide them....*
> *For I am ever a Parent to Israel.* (Jeremiah 31:4–5,
> 31:8–9)

Jeremiah's interest not only in the fact of the ingathering but also in its details—the instruments, the vineyards, the inclusion of his people's most vulnerable—is striking. And it is an interest shared by those who came centuries after him. Postbiblical literature is filled with elaborate, fanciful descriptions of the ingathering of the exiles; as the midrash relates:

> The day on which the exiles will be ingathered is as great as
> the day on which the Torah was given to Israel on Mount

Sinai. And what will be the order of their coming? The
Presence of God shall walk at their head ... and the prophets
at their sides, and the Ark and the Torah will be with them.
And all Israel will be clothed in splendor and wrapped in
great honor, and their radiance will shine from one end of
the world to the other.[21]

And yes, our ancestors were well aware of the challenges posed by
such a monumental assembly; ever practical, the famed medieval
commentator Rashi observed, "The day of the ingathering of the
exiles ... will come about with difficulty, as though God will be
obliged to grasp each one actually by the hand, each one from
their place."[22]

Although Jeremiah and his fellow prophets saw it as a single
and discrete event, by the time of the Talmud the ingathering of
the exiles was understood as an essential feature of the greater
Messianic Age. And for Jewish mystics, this ingathering took on
literally cosmic proportions.

According to Jewish tradition, when our ancestors were exiled
from the Land, the *Shechinah*—the Divine Presence, a feminine
aspect of God—went into exile as well. Mystical teaching came to
identify the *Shechinah* as God's spouse and to envision her as lonely,
devastated, fervently waiting to be reconciled with her lover—that
is, with the male aspect of God. As long as exile persists for God's
people, so too does exile persist for God; for the *Shechinah* can
return to Israel—and to God—only when the ingathering of the
exiles is complete. *Only when the exiles are fully and perfectly restored
will God's nature be fully and perfectly restored as well.*

We who live contentedly in the Diaspora may not consider
ourselves exiles. And we who base our lives more on rationality
and realism than marvels and miracles may not hearken to our
ancestors' dream of returning to Israel "clothed in splendor
and wrapped in great honor." Yet there is something amazing
about the idea, isn't there? For a moment, imagine millions of
Jews, beaming and radiant, making their proud way through
once-menacing or indifferent lands, led and protected by the

Eternal God. Imagine going to a place where there can be no
muttered slurs or subtle discrimination, no shootings or beat-
ings, no bombings or hijackings, no gas chambers or cattle
cars. Imagine going to a country that promises safety and wel-
comes unconditionally. Imagine returning to a Land that feels
like home.

What Is the Relationship between the State of Israel and the Messiah?

Israel's national anthem "*Hatikvah*" captures it perfectly:

> So long as still within the inmost heart a Jewish spirit sings,
> so long as the eye looks eastward, gazing toward Zion, our
> hope is not lost—that hope of two millennia: to be a free
> people in our land, the land of Zion and Jerusalem."[23]

With the return of Jewish rule to Israel, we—and some of our
ancestors—might feel this hope has been fulfilled; but for those
who wait for the traditional Messiah, there is still more to come.

If our ancestors' yearning for Israel were simply a desire to
live free in the Land, the founding of modern Israel would have
satisfied us completely. But, as we have seen, a return to Israel is
but one aspect of the messianic dream.[24] According to tradition,
Jewish sovereignty in Israel would be restored only with the arrival
of the Messiah and would be accompanied by Davidic rule, the full
ingathering of exiles, and the establishment of God's dominion.
In fact, the Messiah and Israel were so inextricably linked that
the notion of Israel without the Messiah was virtually beyond our
ancestors' imagination.

Yet in 1948, that is exactly what happened. Rather than the
Messiah leading his triumphant followers to the Land, the people declared the state's independence. Rather than anointing a
descendant of David king, the people appointed a prime minister and a president. And rather than rebuilding the Temple and
reinstituting traditional law, the people organized a democratic
government and composed a secular constitution.

Israel was in the hands of Jews, but not in the hand of the Messiah. And how we feel about this phenomenon determines how we understand the relationship between the State of Israel and the Messiah.

For some, of course, the issue is entirely irrelevant. We might, after all, regard Israel as a wonder in and of itself: here is a Jewish homeland revived in our ancient borders, a haven for the persecuted, a power that thrives among bitter enemies, a center of science, medicine, education, and literature. Even if we do not ascribe any theological significance to the State of Israel, we still find plenty at which to marvel.

Yet so many attribute the state's founding to an act of God—and, really, it's hard to blame them. How could we not see God's hand in Israel; how could we not sense religious meaning in the return of Jewish rule to the Land after thousands of years? Even President Harry Truman—a supporter of Zionism and the first head of state to recognize Israel—wept when Israel's chief rabbi told him in 1949, "God put you in your mother's womb so that you could be the instrument to bring about the rebirth of Israel."[25] The spirit of this statement beautifully encapsulates religious Zionism—a movement that credits the state's success to the will of God and envisions building up Israel as a true *mitzvah*, a sacred commandment. In the words of Rav Kook, the first chief rabbi of Jerusalem, "Seeing that the Eternal God has chosen Zion, how can one not be a Zionist?"[26]

And how, some might add, can the Jewish restoration of Israel not portend a still greater event—the coming of the Messiah? Perhaps Israel was reborn under different circumstances than our ancestors had expected; perhaps she was reclaimed by the Jews before the actual arrival of the Messiah—but surely Israel serves as *resheit tz'michat ge'ulateinu*, "the foretaste of our messianic redemption." As Zevi Hirsch Kalischer, a nineteenth-century rabbi and Talmudic scholar, explained:

> The Redemption of Israel for which we long is not to be imagined as a sudden miracle.... [God] will not send the

Messiah from heaven in the twinkling of an eye.... On the contrary, the Redemption will begin by awakening support among the philanthropists and by ... the gathering of some of the scattered of Israel into the Holy Land.... As we bring redemption to the land in a "this worldly" way, the rays of heavenly deliverance will gradually appear.[27]

Buttressing this link between the State of Israel and the Messiah was Rabbi Judah Loew ben Bezalel's sixteenth-century prediction that a secular Jewish nation would precede the Messiah's arrival and apocalyptic literature's assertion that the Hebrew language would be revived in the messianic time.[28]

There is, however, another side to this issue. For some Jews awaiting the Messiah, the State of Israel provokes a very different response: it is at best irrelevant and at worst blasphemous. While it may be tempting, they argue, to equate the birth of modern Israel with the miracles to be performed in the time of the Messiah, it is also utterly wrong. To do so is to renounce the other aspects of messianism—the supernatural, the irrational, even the violent elements[29]—that are as essential as they are discomfiting. And the fact that except for the founding of the State of Israel, our world lurches along as wanting and as imperfect as it always has clearly— and sadly—demonstrates that the Messianic Age has yet to begin. Some extremist Jews even refuse to recognize the legitimacy of the State of Israel; without the Messiah, they regard Jewish sovereignty over the Land, particularly in the form of a secular government, as an abomination.

So what is the relationship between the State of Israel and the Messiah? There are many answers, but none is decisive. But neither is any more exhilarating than that of Theodor Herzl, the otherwise stubbornly secular and pragmatic inspiration for the creation of the Jewish state, and he shall have the last word:

One night, I had a wonderful dream. King Messiah came, and he was old and glorious. He lifted me in his arms, and he soared with me on the wings of the wind. On one of the clouds, full of splendor, we met the figure of Moses, and the Messiah called to Moses: "For this child I have prayed!" Then he turned to me: "Go and announce to the Jews that I will soon come and perform great miracles for my people and for the whole world!" I woke up, and it was a dream. I kept this dream a secret and did not dare to tell it to anybody.[30]

How Did the Messiah Become Associated with Supernatural Elements?

The messiahs of the Bible—King Saul, King David, and the Persian king Cyrus—are remarkable people, but they are only people. They possess no superhuman characteristics, and their achievements are confined to this world. Similarly, the descendant of David our biblical prophets so passionately awaited was to be a human being—an amazing human being, but a human being nonetheless. He would be born as anyone else was born, restore his people and his throne to the Land, then die as anyone else would die. During his life and after his death, the universe would continue to function as it always had; his reign would not alter natural law, nor bridge the boundary between heaven and earth. His impact would be limited to the fortunes of Israel.

In postbiblical times, this all changed dramatically. Our ancestors began to anticipate a superhuman Messiah and a Messianic Age of supernatural proportions. The Messiah would not only battle with courage and rule with justice, he would possess otherworldly strength and judgment. And the Messianic Age would mark not only the redemption of Israel from her enemies, but the redemption of the whole universe from evil.

This evolution arose from the trials our ancestors faced and the defeats and persecutions they endured. But it also arose from the tantalizing images they found in the Bible.

While the biblical prophets indeed appeared to anticipate a historical redemption—one that would take place solely within the natural world and within the limits of natural law—still their oracles offered ample hope for those who sought something of a more cosmic significance. Let us look, for example, at the eleventh chapter of Isaiah. Scholars admonish that Isaiah's words refer to a human being and that his evocative language is simply metaphor. But who could fault our ancestors for imagining more when they read the following description?

> *The spirit of the Eternal shall alight upon him....*
> *He shall strike down the ruthless with the rod of his*
>   *mouth,*
> *And slay the wicked with the breath of his lips....*
> *The wolf shall dwell with the lamb, the leopard lie*
>   *down with the kid,*
> *The calf and the beast of prey shall feed together, with*
>   *a little child to lead them....*
> *A babe shall play over a viper's hole, an infant pass*
>   *his hand over the adder's den.*
> *In all of My sacred mount nothing evil or vile shall*
>   *be done,*
> *For the Land shall be filled with devotion to God, as*
>   *the water covers the sea.* (Isaiah 11:2, 11:4, 11:6,
>   11:8–9)

And within the Bible our ancestors even found the book of Daniel, an apocalypse—that is, a work purporting to reveal knowledge about the future and, especially, about the end of the world—that would serve as the basis for countless Jews to calculate the year of the Messiah's arrival. After an evil foreign king "exalts and magnifies himself above every god, and speaks awful things against the God of gods," Daniel relates,

> it will be a time of trouble, the like of which has never been since the nation came into being. At that time your people will be rescued.... Many of those that sleep in the dust of the earth will awake, some to eternal life, others to reproaches, to everlasting abhorrence. And the knowledgeable will be radiant like the bright expanse of sky, and those who lead the many to righteousness will be like the stars forever and ever. (Daniel 11:36, 12:1–3)

The parallels to the resurrection of the dead and the Day of Judgment—two supernatural elements of the Messianic Age we will examine in later chapters—are unmistakable.

These superhuman and supernatural images inspired our ancestors, who had been disappointed time and again by the ostensible redemptions wrought by human beings. When King Cyrus conquered Babylonia and allowed the Jewish exiles to return to Jerusalem and rebuild the Temple, it seemed deliverance had arrived, but the difficult conditions of life in the Land and the eventual subjugation of the Jews to the Syrian-Greek nation proved otherwise. When Judah Maccabee and his brothers defeated the Syrian-Greek armies and liberated the Temple, our ancestors imagined once again that salvation was at hand, but intra-religious strife and infighting led to the Land's occupation by Rome and more centuries of hardship and oppression. Leaders came and went, but problems endured; and the persistence of persecution and imperfection made clear that no purely human being—no matter how capable or charismatic—could possibly bring about the full and complete redemption for which our ancestors yearned.

This sentiment rang especially true after the collapse of the Bar Kochba Revolt in 135 CE. Although not a descendant of King David, Bar Kochba was proclaimed by some Jews to be the Messiah, and when he launched a rebellion against the occupying Romans, his supporters fully expected victory and vindication. The campaign failed horribly, however, leading to terrible punishments and sufferings for the Jewish people. The episode underscored the danger—and the disillusionment—of trusting in a human Messiah and fueled the belief that the real Messiah would be an unmistakably superhuman figure possessing supernatural powers. The ancient Rabbis generally encouraged this perspective, hoping to prevent another would-be human redeemer from attempting to overthrow Rome—and bringing more devastating consequences if he failed.

The transition from a human to a superhuman Messiah also went along quite nicely with the expanding role and tasks with which the Messiah was identified. As early as the Babylonian Exile, our ancestors came to associate God not only with the Land of Israel but with the entire world. Cut off from their Temple, their Land, and the religious customs they had practiced there, our ancestors began to relate to God as we do: as a universal God, present and active in the whole world. While God's primary realm may remain the Land, and God's primary interest the destiny of those who dwelt there, God's reach, God's hand, is to be felt everywhere and among all people.

So when God brought the Messiah, his arrival was to be experienced not only by the Jews, not only in Israel, but by all humanity and in all nations. The Messiah would extend his reign to every corner of the world. His victory over Israel's oppressors would vanquish the forces of evil, his righteous judgment would encompass all God's creatures, his peace would literally unite earth and heaven. *The redeemer of Israel would become no less than the redeemer of the universe.*

But clearly no ordinary person could redeem the universe. In order to carry out his expanded mission, the Messiah would require expanded qualities. He would need to be more than flesh and blood. He would need to be larger than life. He would need to be superhuman.

CHAPTER THREE

The Messiah
Is a Warrior

The Messianic Age promises unparalleled abundance and prosperity, perfect justice and peace. All the more striking, then, is the contrast between this era and what will precede it: devastating wars and bloodshed, bitter betrayal and dishonor—the complete breakdown of all our ancestors knew and cherished.

Terrifying images of violent battles and shameful defeat pervaded the oracles of our biblical prophets; only after these trials, they taught, would God grant Israel triumph and redemption. And while we might expect later messianists to overlook or explain away these disturbing visions, some in fact did quite the opposite. The tumult, the catastrophe, the mayhem that would characterize the time before the Messiah captured their imaginations; it echoed their own experiences of persecution and humiliation and inspired them to produce ever-more detailed and elaborate descriptions of the frightful days in whose wake the Messiah would arrive.

What is contained in these accounts? What wisdom do they hold, and how do they enable us to understand the fears that tormented our ancestors and the hopes that sustained them? What is their meaning for Jewish tradition—and for us today?

Out of this challenging, amazing, stirring, and baffling literature comes an essential facet of our understanding of the Messiah:
If, as we have learned, the Messiah was to be an instrument of
universal and supernatural change, such change would not come
easily or peacefully. *Such a violent break with all that the world had
ever experienced could only be accomplished violently*—with combat and
suffering, with awe and dread. To face such anguish, and to guide
his people—indeed, the entire universe—through it would be a
mighty task.

As we have seen, the Messiah could be no ordinary man.
Nor, we see now, could he be only a man of charisma, or wisdom,
or peace.

The Messiah would be a warrior.

What Will the World Be Like Just Before the Messiah Comes?

The linking of calamity with redemption is as old as the Torah.
The seminal events of Israelite history—the parting of the Red Sea
and the Revelation at Mount Sinai—were preceded by four hundred years of slavery and degradation in Egypt, and in the book of
Deuteronomy we learn that this pattern is enduring. Before God
delivers us, Moses warns,

> Will the Eternal scatter you among all the peoples from one
> end of the earth to the other.... Yet even among those nations
> you shall find no peace, nor shall your foot find a place to
> rest. The Eternal will give you there an anguished heart and
> eyes that pine and a despondent spirit. The life you face shall
> be precarious; you shall be in terror, night and day, with no
> assurance of survival. In the morning you shall say, "If only
> it were evening!" and in the evening you shall say, "If only it
> were morning!"—because of what your heart shall dread and
> your eyes shall see. (Deuteronomy 28:64–67)[1]

The visions of our biblical prophets reinforce this theme. Although
these men lived and prophesized in different lands and eras and

under radically different circumstances from each other, not a single one promised redemption and triumph without suffering and humiliation. Amos offers a chilling—but not atypical—example: The sun will set at noon, he tells, and the earth will grow dark on a sunny day. Festivals will turn into mourning, and songs to dirges; the earth itself will mourn, "as for an only child, all of it as on a bitter day" (Amos 8:9–10). Yet in the very next chapter, Amos predicts God's fulfillment of the messianic promise: "I will set up again the fallen booth of David," God proclaims. "I will restore My people Israel ... and I will plant them upon their soil, nevermore to be uprooted from the soil I have given them" (Amos 9:11, 9:14–15).

According to the Bible, then, the days before our redemption will be marked by national catastrophe and sinister changes in the natural world. And, the Talmud cautions, we will not find solace from one another; the chaos will corrupt even the sacred units of Jewish society and family:

> Arrogance will increase, prices will rise, grapes will be abundant—but wine will be costly. The government will turn into heresy, and there will be no reproach. The meeting place [of scholars] will become a bordello ... sin-fearing people will be detested ... young men will humiliate the elderly.... Sons will revile their fathers, daughters will strike their mothers ... and children will have no shame before their parents.[2]

The anguish is to be absolute and complete. For these are but examples; images of warfare and exile, famine and bloodshed, bewilderment and terror fill our most sacred texts. Our sages came to call these ordeals *chevlei Mashiach*, "the birth pangs of the Messiah"—just as a mother's painful labor concludes with the birth of a child, they taught, so would Israel's distress culminate in the arrival of her redeemer. (First found in the Talmud, this term proved incredibly enduring; for over fifteen hundred years it has been applied to episodes of suffering by Jews hopeful that their trials signaled the Messiah's imminence.) And while accounts differ on the details of our misery, they are united on one clear message: our despair would be so tremendous, the calamity so endemic, that we would find no relief in this world. As the Talmudic passage we just read concludes, "To whom can one turn? Only to our Parent in heaven."[3]

"To whom can one turn? Only to our Parent in heaven"—that, according to traditional messianic belief, is precisely the point.

For what is the purpose of all this suffering? We might posit that it will make the Messianic Age all the sweeter, or that it is a horrible but necessary tool to bring about such a dramatic break with all that had come before, or that these terrible images reflect the tribulations our ancestors had already borne—and that they feared still awaited them. Jewish tradition, however, adds another—and infinitely more disturbing—rationale: Redemption is given only as a reward for repentance and righteousness. If people are living comfortable and secure, they will not repent or behave righteously. Therefore, God unleashes these *chevlei Mashiach*, these birth pangs of the Messiah, upon Israel in order to move us to repentance and righteousness—so that God can in turn bring the Messianic Age.

Although this view occupies a prominent role in traditional Jewish thought and theology, it has almost always been passionately challenged. It may bring solace to some; we may more easily accept our trials if we imagine that they have some higher meaning and if we see them not as random and potentially limitless, but as deserved and to be ended when they have achieved their purpose. Still, the idea that suffering and cruelty are necessary preconditions to divine favor is more likely anathema to our understanding of the universe—and of God. And after a millennium that began with the massacre of Jewish communities during the Crusades and ended in the Holocaust—but that did not bring the Messiah—how can we possibly say that our people must suffer even more to merit redemption?

We may be gratified to see our misgivings rooted squarely in Jewish tradition. Even fifteen hundred years ago some of our great Rabbinic sages—who were well acquainted with affliction and exile, persecution and slaughter—sought to sever the connection among suffering, repentance, and the arrival of the Messiah. They declared that God would bring the Messiah at an appointed time, not according to the behavior of that era's Jews, but according to God's ultimate plan for the universe.

While the Messiah's advent might indeed involve violence and bloodshed, these need not be interpreted as motivators for repentance nor as indictments of the Jewish people.

What Is Apocalyptic Literature?

An apocalypse, the End of Days, wars of the Lord—these may not be phrases we associate with Jewish tradition. Yet the concepts originated in Judaism, and although they found eager audiences among early Christians—not to mention modern evangelicals—they also inspired and enthralled generations of Jews who sought the Messiah.

Apocalyptic literature provides a marvelous record of their quest. The term "apocalyptic literature" refers to accounts of secret or esoteric knowledge, usually related to the workings of heaven or the End of Days, ostensibly revealed by God or the angels. (Because the authors of apocalypses wrote not as themselves but in the persona of ancient figures—lending credibility to their often wild tales by ascribing them to revered patriarchs like Abraham, Moses, or Rabbi Akiva—early examples of this genre are also known as "pseudepigrapha," which literally means "false title.") These amazing works are informed by the biblical prophets' descriptions of the tremendous suffering and ferocious battles that await us in the days before redemption, but apocalyptic literature takes these depictions to new heights. Combining expertise in traditional scripture, insight into Jewish history, and perhaps most of all, vivid imagination, stunning creativity, and captivating language, apocalyptic writers crafted literature that fascinates to this day.

Although we who remember the hype around the *Left Behind* series and see "Warning! In case of Rapture this car will be unmanned" bumper stickers might understandably associate apocalyptic literature chiefly with Christianity, its roots are actually Jewish. Jews were the first to compose apocalypses and did so beginning in the third century BCE. One apocalypse, the book of Daniel, found its way into the Bible; another, the *War Scroll* contained in the Dead Sea Scrolls, electrified modern scholars with its elaborate depiction of a forty-year battle between the Sons of Light and the Sons of Darkness.[4] Across the ages, apocalyptic authors well understood the traditional link between catastrophe and redemption, and they found in the tumult and upheavals of their eras signs of imminent messianic deliverance. Juxtaposing biblical images with barely veiled references to more recent episodes—during the centuries in which apocalyptic literature flourished, these ranged from the persecutions of the Syrian-Greek king Antiochus and failure of the Bar Kochba Revolt to the political intrigues surrounding the Byzantine Empire and the rise of Islam—these writers created stories of supernatural signs, hideous wars, and unimaginable wonders that were equal parts compelling and horrifying, repulsive and addictive. In addition to exploring the Messianic Age, they also focused on the Messiah himself, bringing to Judaism the first details about our redeemer's personality and appearance.

To make their tales even more persuasive, authors would recast past events as future prophecies of messianic import. There are literally hundreds of examples; here is but one. The composer of the spectacular apocalypse *Sefer Zerubbabel*[5] lived during the seventh century, but he did not set *Sefer Zerubbabel* in the seventh century; rather, he wrote it from the perspective of the biblical Zerubbabel, who had lived over a thousand years earlier. So even though the *author* was well aware of the Second Temple's destruction and the rise of Roman rule, since they had occurred nearly six hundred years before he was born, he wrote from the perspective of someone who knew nothing of these events because they were still far in the future. In *Sefer Zerubbabel*, an angel reveals to Zerubbabel how history will unfold year by year until the Messiah arrives; included in these supposed glimpses into the future are references to the Second Temple's ruin and Rome's ascendance. These were not real prophecies—they were actual past events—but the author made his apocalypse more plausible by presenting them as prophecies entrusted to Zerubbabel. If some of *Sefer Zerubbabel's* "prophecies" had been fulfilled already, a reader might think, surely the rest of them—no matter how far-fetched or improbable—were worthy of belief as well.

And what were the expectations of these apocalyptic authors? In the *Sibylline Oracles*—an early and remarkable apocalypse, reflecting the then-recent triumph of the Maccabees' defeat of the Syrian-Greeks and the restoration of Jewish sovereignty to Jerusalem—the narrator relates:

> When swords in the starlit heaven appear by night towards dusk and towards dawn, and straightway dust is carried from heaven to earth, and all the brightness of the sun fails at midday from the heaven, and the moon's rays shine forth and come back to earth, and a sign comes from the rocks with dripping streams of blood; and in a cloud you shall see a battle of foot and horse, as a hunt of wild beasts, like unto misty clouds. This is the consummation of the war which God, whose dwelling is in heaven, is bringing to pass.[6]

Generations later, in the wake of Rome's overtaking Jerusalem and razing the Temple in 70 CE, another apocalypse, *4 Ezra*, taught:

> When in the world there shall appear quaking of lands, tumult of peoples, schemings of nations, confusion of leaders, disquietude of princes, then thou shalt understand that it is of these things the Most High has spoken.... For just as with respect to all that has happened in the world, it has a beginning in the word (of God at creation) and a manifest end.[7]

But perhaps the finest apocalyptic work is the aforementioned *Sefer Zerubbabel*, which combines earlier messianic traditions with totally original elements to create a chillingly detailed account of the End of Days—and the figures by whose hands our sufferings and redemption will come to pass:

> With their own eyes all the children of Israel will see the Eternal, like a man of war with a helmet of salvation on his head, dressed in armor.... [The enemies of Israel] will all fall dead in the valley of Arbael.[8] ... But a fraction [of the enemy] will escape and gather at Zela ha-Eleph, five hundred men, and a hundred thousand dressed in armor. [Against them] will be five hundred men of Israel, with [the Messiah] at their head. And [you] will kill all of them, for there one man shall pursue a thousand.[9]

These fascinating and brutal, engaging and bloody accounts enjoyed tremendous acclaim in their time.[10] Their writers were likened to "popular prophets"[11]—bringers of wisdom and foresight not necessarily to the privileged and the educated, but to the masses. And it was these masses who most embraced apocalyptic literature; yes, it was often inelegant, or unclear, or convoluted, or just totally preposterous, but it possessed a fierceness of belief, a conviction, that felt true and unshakable and right. And while the elite of various periods—the Mishnah's sages, the medieval philosophers, the Enlightenment's intellectuals—would reject and even censor these apocalypses, the work—and the passion that suffused it—would continue to influence and endure.

Against Whom Will the Messiah Go to War?

Of all the images of *chevlei Mashiach*, the birth pangs of the Messiah, none have held more fascination than those of apocalyptic battles. And in the time of the Bible and the medieval age, we find named particular foes, each bearing particular significance, who will rise against Israel, against the Messiah, and even against God.

The prophet Ezekiel is the first to see the enmity and hatred that will precede redemption embodied in a specific character: "Gog, of the land of Magog, the chief prince of Meshech and Tubal" (Ezekiel 38:2). While certainly influenced by the tumult of his times—Ezekiel lived during the Babylonian Exile, after the destruction of the First Temple and the devastating loss of Jewish sovereignty in the Land—Ezekiel appears to see Gog not as historical but as purely symbolic. Gog does not strike at Israel for political reasons or in hopes of expanding his military kingdom, as the Babylonians had; rather, Gog is motivated only by evil—only by the desire to unleash suffering upon God's people.

And Gog proves a mighty adversary. Speaking of Gog, God proclaims:

> A thought will occur to you, and you will conceive of a wicked design.... You will come from your home in the farthest north, you and many people with you—all of them mounted on horses, a vast horde, a mighty army—and you will advance upon My people Israel, like a cloud covering the earth. This shall happen on that distant day. (Ezekiel 38:11, 38:15–16)

The battle with Gog—linked in the book of Ezekiel with Israel's full and final redemption—took on even greater significance in postbiblical literature. Although Ezekiel depicts God alone fighting Gog, the *Targum* (a translation of the Bible from Hebrew to Aramaic, the language of the Jewish masses) portrays the Messiah as leading the charge.[12] And various apocalypses cite Gog and Magog—later seen not as a place but as an entity, and Gog's partner in evil—among the enemies in the three wars the Messiah is destined to fight.

It would be a thousand years after Ezekiel before apocalyptic literature spawned another compelling foe to challenge Israel in the days before the Messiah. In *Sefer Zerubbabel* we first encounter the figure of Armilus, a creature so terrible, so powerful, and so brilliantly realized that he became nearly ubiquitous in later apocalypses and even earned mention in the great philosopher Saadia Gaon's masterwork *Emunot veDeyot*.[13]

Simply the most basic description of Armilus evokes disgust: "The hair of his head is colored like gold. He is green to the soles of his feet," intones the author of *Sefer Zerubbabel*. "The width of his face is a span. His eyes are deep. He has two heads.... All who see him will tremble."[14] And his deeds match his revolting appearance: in a scenario reminiscent of the Christian Antichrist, Armilus will convince the world of his divinity and take power over all the nations—then wage war upon Israel and drive the defeated Jews into exile and famine.

But in contrast to Ezekiel's Gog, the Armilus of *Sefer Zerubbabel* is firmly founded in history. He represents the worst of Israel's then-contemporary enemies, Rome and Christianity, and this daringly rendered identification lent depth and significance to his character—and to *Sefer Zerubbabel*.

Certainly the destruction of the First Temple and the Babylonian Exile had been traumatic for the Jewish people, as had the second-century-BCE persecutions of King Antiochus. But life under detested Rome—who had conquered Jerusalem, razed the Second Temple, put down the Bar Kochba Revolt with a cruel and heavy hand, and continued to oppress and humiliate the Jews—exceeded all the previous sufferings of our ancestors. The flourishing of a hostile Christianity only added to the burdens. And so there emerges in the literature of these periods a sense that *chevlei Mashiach*, the birth pangs of the Messiah, are not some far-off trials at the hand of a future enemy; rather, they are occurring here and now, orchestrated by the Romans and the Christians.

Where our sages filled the midrash with biting references to Rome, it is *Sefer Zerubbabel* that most clearly captures the scorn and rage with which some apocalyptics regarded Christianity. At the beginning of the work, Zerubbabel is summoned to what God calls "the house of disgrace"[15]—unmistakably a church—in order to learn about Armilus. There an angel shows Zerubbabel "a marble stone in the shape of a virgin ... the beauty of [whose] appearance was wonderful to behold"[16] and explains that this statue, obviously representing Mary, is the mother of Armilus. "This statue is the wife of [the satanic figure] Belial," the angel explains. "Satan will come and lie with her, and she will bear a son named Armilus."[17] It is a total perversion of Christian beliefs and a blasphemous use of their most sacred imagery. Today we might shrink from such language, but first we might do well to remember how our ancestors experienced Christianity. To them, Christians were not kind and welcoming neighbors, and Christianity was not a religion of tolerance and peace. In their time, Christianity had been made into a tool of oppression, humiliation, and even slaughter; surely such a faith, they must have felt, was not of divine origin, but exactly the opposite.

The enduring appeal of Armilus suggests an equally enduring distrust of Christianity. Despite the cruelties it inflicted upon God's supposedly chosen people, Christianity thrived, growing in power and influence and at times all but eclipsing the Judaism from which it had arisen. Personifying this religion as a messianic enemy gave tremendous comfort to our ancestors; what they could not say about Christianity for fear of reprisals they could say about Armilus, and what they could not say explicitly they could communicate obliquely, in the language of apocalypse. It must have given them a measure of pride and hope, and these were surely in short supply when our ancestors believed they were experiencing the birth pangs of the Messiah, but the group responsible for their suffering proclaimed that the Messiah—and the divine love he represented—had already been bequeathed to them.

Who Is the Messiah ben Joseph?

As discussed in chapter 1, the qualities and the tasks of the Messiah are manifold—and sometimes contradictory. The Messiah is mere flesh and blood, totally mortal—and of divine origin and possessed of supernatural powers. The Messiah suffers and sacrifices for us—and enfolds us in his glory. The Messiah is a warrior—and the prince of peace.

How to bridge the chasm between these very different concepts of the Messiah and the very different images they evoke of the Messianic Age? With typical daring and innovation, our ancestors hit upon a radical, but brilliant solution: there must, they decided, be two Messiahs.[18]

This second Messiah—called Messiah ben Joseph,[19] the Messiah descended from our patriarch and matriarch Jacob and Rachel's son Joseph[20]—makes early appearances in the Talmud and midrash and becomes a common feature of apocalyptic literature and later messianic movements. He is a fascinating character, embodying the warrior aspect of the Messiah and serving as a chief protagonist in accounts of the struggles, violence, and bloodshed that mark the End of Days. Although his powers are limited to amazing vigor and prowess in battle—no text endows him with supernatural or otherworldly attributes—the Messiah ben Joseph occupies an essential role in messianic tradition and has proved nearly as spellbinding as his partner and successor, the Messiah ben David, the Messiah descended from King David.

While a variety of narratives sprang up around the Messiah ben Joseph, his destiny generally unfolds as follows: During *chevlei Mashiach*, the terrible days of the birth pangs of the Messiah, the Messiah ben Joseph will reveal himself and galvanize the Jewish people into rising up against their oppressors. He will command the hosts of Israel in combat, overseeing incredible victories, killing the king of Rome, and even restoring to Jewish hands the precious Temple vessels stolen by the Romans, before perishing in battle.[21] Devastation will follow. According to one text, the world will revert to chaos;[22] according to another, Israel will flee into the wilderness and seek protection under divine Clouds of Glory.[23] One recurring and more hopeful motif states that for forty days the Messiah ben Joseph's body will lie in the streets of Jerusalem, untouched—until the Messiah ben David arrives, sees to his resurrection, and ushers in Israel's triumphant redemption.

As far-fetched as a second messianic figure might appear—especially one doomed to die before his work would be complete—our ancestors may have rooted the Messiah ben Joseph in historical reality. The Messiah ben Joseph emerges strongly in the time of the Roman emperor Hadrian, who oversaw Rome's brutal victory over Israel during the Bar Kochba Revolt. And many scholars have noted the parallels between Bar Kochba and depictions of the Messiah ben Joseph: both are charismatic and courageous warriors, battling strong and hateful enemies, and both fall to their foes rather than lead their nations to victory. Our ancestors' enduring embrace of the Messiah ben Joseph may testify not only to the power Bar Kochba's memory exerted upon them, but also to the tragic fact that many generations witnessed the failures and deaths of those they hoped would achieve victory and deliverance.[24] Rather than seeing aborted messianic hopes as devastating failures, our ancestors could interpret them as manifestations of the Messiah ben Joseph—and as indications that the Messiah ben David was well on his way.

According to some, however, the foundation of the Messiah ben Joseph is even older. The Bible hints that two different figures will play important roles in Israel's redemption. During the Second Temple period, the prophet Zechariah offered an oracle about the people of Jerusalem "lamenting to [God] about those who are slain ... showing bitter grief as over a firstborn" (Zechariah 12:10). The book of Daniel also contains a cryptic reference to "an anointed one [who] will disappear and vanish" (Daniel 9:26). These fallen would-be heroes came to be identified with the Messiah ben Joseph. Another scholar theorizes that the Messiah ben Joseph might even parallel Moses's successor Joshua, a fellow descendant of Joseph credited with bringing the Holy Land into Israelite hands.[25]

But for all of his noble origins and compelling deeds, the Messiah ben Joseph remains always—and necessarily—subordinate to the Messiah ben David. Their lineages reflect this fact—Joseph gave rise to only the humble tribe of Ephraim and the half-tribe of Manasseh, while David comes from the lofty tribe of Judah—and, more clearly, so do their tasks. Where the bloody work of warfare falls to the Messiah ben Joseph, the Messiah ben David is entrusted with the most celebrated features of the Messianic Age: the establishment of justice and peace, universal worship of God, the creation of an entirely new and perfectly ordered universe. It is only with the death of the Messiah ben Joseph—and the end

of the suffering he personifies—that the Messiah ben David—and
the glorious redemption he represents—can live.

Who Is Hephzibah?

The world of the Messiah appears to be a man's world. Although
women will fully experience the horrors of *chevlei Mashiach*, the
birth pangs of the Messiah, as well as the joys and wonders of the
Messianic Age, they usually stand far off to the side, witnessing
rather than guiding the action. Almost all of the players in apocalyptic literature, including the Messiah himself, are male.

A thankful exception is the figure of Hephzibah.

Appearing most significantly in *Sefer Zerubbabel*, Hephzibah
would be a welcome addition to the cast of messianic characters
regardless of gender. She is brave and noble, questing and deter-
mined. And although she bears the honored title of mother of the
Messiah, she is distinguished as much by her own deeds as by her
offspring.

Hephzibah's very name conveys her importance. The Bible
records that a wife of King Hezekiah—the post-Davidic monarch most closely associated with the Messiah—was also called
Hephzibah (2 Kings 21:1); and "Hephzibah," translated as "my
delight is in her," is how God promises Isaiah the Jewish people
shall be known in the days of our redemption (Isaiah 62:4). And in
Sefer Zerubbabel, the figure of Hephzibah holds an essential role in
achieving that redemption: during the messianic wars, Hephzibah
will fight alongside the Messiah ben Joseph, slaying two kings and,
after the Messiah ben Joseph falls to Armilus, stationing herself at
Jerusalem's east gate and saving the city from an enemy onslaught.

Hephzibah is empowered in these battles by an amazing and
enigmatic tool: the "staff of wonders," which God assigns to her
specifically. This staff, according to *Sefer Zerubbabel*, "is made of
almond wood, and it is hidden away in Rakkath, a city in Naphtali.
This is the staff that the Lord gave Adam and Moses and Aaron
and Joshua and King David; it is the staff that blossomed and
sprouted in the tent [of] Aaron."[26] These descriptions draw on

an ancient tradition that from the time of Creation, a sacred staff had been handed down among God's chosen; then it was divinely hidden away, not to be used again until the approach of the End of Days. This was the same staff Moses grasped when he beheld the Burning Bush, the same staff that God turned into a serpent to prove the divine might to Pharaoh in Egypt. For the author of *Sefer Zerubbabel* to place this staff in the hand of Hephzibah—in the hand of a woman—was extremely daring and extremely provocative. And Hephzibah holds this staff until redemption is nearly complete; she releases it only to her son—the Messiah ben David—when he reveals himself at the gate of Jerusalem.

And Hephzibah wields the staff well. *Sefer Zerubbabel* tells:

> In the fifth year of [the Messiah ben Joseph][27] and the gathering of the holy ones, Shiroi, king of Persia, will go up against [the Messiah ben Joseph] and Israel, and there will be great trouble for Israel. Hephzibah ... the mother of [the Messiah ben David][28] will go out with the staff that the Lord God of Israel gave her. And the Lord will make a spirit of confusion enter [Israel's enemies], and they will slay one another, and there the wicked will die.[29]

Hephzibah's victory marks the first of three apocalyptic battles; the second will be won by the Messiah ben Joseph, and the third by God, fighting alongside the Messiah ben David.[30]

Though Hephzibah stands unique in both her prominence and her acts, she is not the only Jewish woman in apocalyptic tradition. Several other female characters are mentioned in messianic texts; however, all surface very briefly and are discussed only as they relate directly to the Messiah. Their appearances, therefore, prove less than satisfying. For example, in recounting the legend that the Messiah was born on the same day as the Temple's destruction, then snatched up to heaven in a storm to wait until the appointed time of his arrival, the midrash halfheartedly explores the reaction of his mother: "Did I not tell you that his luck was bad?" she complains. "On the day on which he was born the Temple was

destroyed.... Then a wind bore down upon him from the four corners of the world and blew him into the great sea."[31] Although we
might expect the mother to express her presumed grief and bewilderment in striking words or actions, we are not privy to them;
her role in the story ends here.[32] Not even the *Shechinah*—the
feminine aspect of God, often understood as the Divine Presence
itself—receives more attention; while the *Zohar* intriguingly asserts
that the *Shechinah* birthed the Messiah, the explanation centers on
the pain of labor and the mechanics of delivery ("her womb con-
sists of two houses—to give birth to two Messiahs"[33]) rather than
the emotional and spiritual implications of such an event.

In this environment, it is perhaps not surprising that the figure of Hephzibah did not endure. As influential and pervasive as
Sefer Zerubbabel proved to be, Hephzibah never appeared again.
Even texts that expressly modeled themselves on *Sefer Zerubbabel*
chose to excise her role completely. A female warrior—a woman
taking a huge role in Israel's redemptive drama—proved unable
to hold the interest or, more likely, to earn the approval of those
who wrote and devoured apocalyptic literature.

Hephzibah, clearly, was an anomaly. And while it may not be
hard to understand how her character died out, it is still fascinating to wonder how she arose in the first place. Scholars speculate
as well, positing that Hephzibah was inspired by a female-led rebellion in Jerusalem, or intended as a foil to Christianity's vaunted
feminine figure, the Virgin Mary, or simply conceived by an ahead-
of-his-time visionary. No definitive evidence exists for any of these
possibilities; all we know is that Hephzibah was indeed created and
that messianic tradition—and we who study it—are richer for it.

How Will the Messiah Triumph?

And now we turn to the climax of these climactic battles: The
(oh so) long-awaited entrance—and triumph—of the ultimate
Messiah, the Messiah of the House of David.

His arrival is heralded in vivid, breathless prose. Texts from
various eras and reflecting myriad literary and historical influences

are united in an awestruck promise: the Messiah shall prove a warrior like no other. One midrashic collection asserts that among the Messiah's seven names is the appellation *Gibbor*, "Hero."[34] "Amiel," the name by which the medieval apocalypse *Sefer Zerubbabel* knows the father of the Messiah, shares the same *gematria*, or numerical value, as *gana*, "vengeance."[35] According to Jewish interpretations of *gematria*—which finds links between seemingly unrelated words based on the numerical values of their letters—a thirst for vengeance, then, is an essential component of the Messiah. And the *Zohar* envisions "the King Messiah ... girded with his weapons" and crowned with the exact same crown of war that adorned the Divine Presence at the parting of the Red Sea and the drowning of the hosts of Egypt.[36]

And the actions of the Messiah fulfill these enormous expectations, as the horrors of *chevlei Mashiach*, the birth pangs of the Messiah, yield at last to otherworldly glories. In the apocalyptics' hands, our biblical prophets' allusions to redemptive battles took on cosmic significance; taken quite literally, for example, was God's promise to Zechariah that on the day of salvation, "in that day, the Eternal will shield the inhabitants of Jerusalem; and the feeblest of them shall be in that day like David, and the House of David like a divine being, like an angel of the Eternal" (Zechariah 12:8).

And like an avenging angel, the apocalyptics' Messiah would unleash his power against the enemies of Israel. Recounts the narrator of the pseudepigraphic *4 Ezra*:

> [He] neither lifted his hand, nor held spear nor any warlike weapon, but I saw only as he sent out of his mouth as it were a fiery stream, and out of his lips a flaming breath, and out of his tongue he shot forth a storm of sparks. And these were all mingled together—the fiery stream, the flaming breath, and the great storm [of sparks]—and fell mightily upon the multitude which was prepared to fight, and burned them all up; so that suddenly nothing more was to be seen of the innumerable multitude save only dust of ashes and smell of smoke.[37]

A similar image appears in *Sefer Zerubbabel,* where the Messiah "will breathe on Armilus with his nostrils and slay him."[38] As the acclaimed modern scholar Gershom Scholem characterizes these mighty acts, the Messiah "is the one in whom what is new finally comes to the fore, who once and for all defeats the antichrist."[39]

But even amid the praise and excitement, one thing remains always clear: for all of the Messiah's splendor, he depends upon God for his grandeur and for his ultimate triumph. The Messiah is, to be sure, God's agent, but he is not God's incarnation; we may pray *for* the Messiah, but we may not pray *to* him. As awesome as the Messiah shall be, God is ever so much more so, rightly demanding our foremost loyalty and reverence. In unambiguous rebuke to Christianity, even the most impassioned Jewish messianists proclaim: There can be only one truly divine being—and it is not one who takes the form of a man.

For the Messiah does not triumph alone. Not only is his victory founded on the courageous actions of his predecessor the Messiah ben Joseph, but even upon his advent, the Messiah ben David relies on two of the most powerful figures in Jewish tradition: God, of course, and also the prophet Elijah.

We will learn in chapter 5 of Elijah's role in announcing the Messiah and ushering in the End of Days, but some traditions credit him with essential contributions to the messianic wars as well. The biblical book of Kings portrays Elijah as an almost fanatical witness to the Divine, recording bloody battles he waged for God's honor; surely this aspect of Elijah inspired accounts like this one: "The Holy One, blessed be God, will seize [Rome's celestial] prince by the lock of his head, and Elijah will slaughter him, and his blood is dashed at his garments as he returns."[40]

But of course it is God who—even during the Messiah's magnificent reign—remains the central figure. Even the most starry-eyed apocalyptic authors note that the Messiah's conquests depend on God's direct intervention and are overshadowed by it. After narrating the Messiah's amazing success over Armilus, for example, *Sefer Zerubbabel* turns almost immediately to describing God's more significant defeat of Israel's ancient foes Gog and Magog. And in a passage from the influential text *Otot HaMashiach* ("Signs of the Messiah"), God explicitly affirms the totality of divine power, instructing the Messiah, "'Sit on My right!' And God will say to Israel: 'Stay and see the salvation of the Eternal which *God* will perform for you today!'"[41]

And yet it is virtually impossible to remain unmoved by the figure of the Messiah and irresistible to anticipate and savor his feats. For the scope of the Messiah's victory is not limited to the military, political, or even the natural realm. Fighting alongside God, he vanquishes not only the enemies of Israel, but all enmity toward Israel. He subdues not only evil men, but evil itself. And he achieves a triumph that dwarfs every other triumph in history and even history itself, for only by his triumph is the universe born—or, perhaps, reborn—as something we can only imagine.

In the words of the Talmud, "War is the beginning of redemption."[42] And the culmination of this war is indeed redemption: redemption not only from our sufferings in this world, but from this world itself.

CHAPTER FOUR

The Messiah Will Change Everything

We find two essential—but contradictory—elements in Jewish messianism: Our redemption will perfect the world as we know it. And our redemption will destroy the world as we know it.

With the Messiah will come justice, and plenty, and peace—the perfection of our universe. But the universe as it exists now cannot possibly know such goodness, such grandeur. In order to reach its potential—in order to prove a worthy dwelling place of the Messiah and the nation God instructed him to redeem—the universe must change, fully, fundamentally, even violently. The universe we know must be destroyed, so that we might come to know the universe perfected.

In the years before the Messiah's arrival, Jewish tradition teaches, the world will indeed know tumult and upheaval. Faithlessness and strife, war and want, hardship and suffering will shatter our understanding of how the universe operates. Amid the birth pangs of the Messiah, the natural world, society and community, even humanity itself will dissolve into chaos; everything will change for the worse.

The advent of the Messiah does not end this change; it only, we might say, changes it. With the Messiah, everything changes for the better. Enmity, evil, and subjugation are no more; all barriers

57

to fulfilling our capacity for goodness are removed; redemption from every trial is at hand. We return to the magnificent innocence of Creation, before we learned separateness and disobedience, conflict and betrayal. We are restored to the time when God saw everything, and proclaimed it "very good" (Genesis 1:31).

We can hardly imagine such a deliverance; certainly the world in which we have labored, and anguished, and endured cannot contain it. Our redemption, then, can only unfold in a new world— a place where we experience nature, ourselves, one another, and even God in an entirely new way. But what will such a universe be like? By what process can we bridge the chasm between catastrophe and redemption, between the world that is and the world that shall be?

Our ancestors embraced these questions, and their responses reflect myriad worldviews, circumstances, and philosophies. Some of their ideas are rational, some outlandish; some compelling, some seemingly insane. We will not accept them all or even most, but we may find ourselves moved by most, if not all. For each of their teachings offers a taste of the excitement of an entirely new world—a sense of exhilarating freedom, the tantalizing promise of being finally redeemed and reborn.

How Will the Natural World Be Different in the Days of the Messiah?

The triumph of the Messiah, Jewish teaching promises, will end not only the reign of evil humans, but the reign of human evil. With the defeat of Israel's foes comes the defeat of enmity itself, of the injustice and cruelty and causeless hatred that for so long stained the divine creation.

This would be awesome enough. But there is much more.

For the evil perpetrated by humanity is, of course, not the only malevolence in the world. Nature itself proves a source of evil: of roiling earthquakes and fierce windstorms, marauding beasts who prey upon the weak, drought and fire, flood and famine. Even once redeemed from our own wickedness, still we might stand helpless in the face of nature's brutal indifference to us and to our needs.

But according to ancient Judaism, human evil and natural evil are irrevocably linked. While many contemporaneous faiths envisaged the forces of nature as divine powers and sought to tame them through rituals or incantations, the Torah maintains that our relationship with nature is based strictly on ethics: what we do determines what nature does to us. "If you do not obey the Eternal your God, and observe faithfully all God's commandments and laws," warns the book of Deuteronomy, "cursed will be ... the produce of your soil, the calving of your herd and the lambing of your flock" (28:15, 28:18). Our wickedness will lead to "scorching heat and drought, with blight and mildew" (28:22). Rain will turn to dust, "and sand shall drop on you from the sky, until you are wiped out" (28:34). For our ancestors, natural evil was a reflection of human evil—never part of God's plan, but brought into being by our sins.

So in our redemption from human iniquity, messianic tradition teaches, we are also delivered from the iniquity of nature. Freed of our transgression, the natural world can reclaim the beautiful and benevolent character with which God endowed it; unhindered by human evil, nature can once again flourish as God intended. And imagining this glorious restoration of the natural world, reborn in the age of the Messiah and in the image of God, delighted our ancestors. Seizing on the promises of the biblical prophets, who filled their oracles with images and metaphors of natural abundance, sages, mystics, and apocalyptics portrayed a world completely transformed.

Fertility and harvests will be magnified incredibly, they taught. A single grape will yield thirty kegs of wine,[1] crops will ripen every fifteen days,[2] wheat will grow higher than mountaintops.[3]

> There will be no vinestock in the Land of Israel which will not require a whole city to harvest it. And there will be no shade tree in the Land of Israel which will not produce a load of fruit for two donkeys ... and think not that the fruits

will have no wine in them, or that it will not be red, or that it will not refresh, or that it will have no taste, or that it will not be equally suited for youths and for [the] old.[4]

And as we will discuss in the next section, this phenomenon will even extend to humanity: "Each one in Israel," one midrash predicts, "will beget children every day."[5]

In the Messianic Age, we will find the animal kingdom changed as well, but to understand the significance of this change, we must go all the way back to the beginning. When God created the world and placed Adam and Eve in the Garden of Eden, we were expected to eat only the fruit of the earth—that is, to follow a strictly vegetarian diet—and to live in harmony with all animals. It was only after the Flood, only after humanity had immersed ourselves in wickedness and proved unable to meet God's lofty expectations for us, that we were permitted to eat meat. Therefore, some messianists explain, once we have overcome our capacity for evil, we will easily return to vegetarianism—and will heal our relationship with the animal world. With the advent of the Messiah, one tradition teaches, once-dangerous beasts will continue to exist but will "cease from doing harm."[6] "Beasts only prey [on human beings] on account of the sin of [humanity]," the thirteenth-century rabbi and physician Moses ben Nachman, or Nachmanides, reasoned. "But ... when [humanity will be] in a state of perfection, [they] will cease from their harmful way."[7] So trusting will animals become, the midrash promises, "that in the future a babe in Israel will stick his finger into the eyeball of a basilisk and will extract gall from its mouth."[8] Animals will even treat one another peaceably in the age of redemption; a literal interpretation of the prophet Isaiah's words invokes a time when "the wolf shall dwell with the lamb, the leopard lie down with the kid, the calf the beast of prey, and the fatling together.... The cow and the bear shall graze, their young shall lie down together; and the lion, like the ox, shall eat straw" (Isaiah 11:6–7).

These depictions capture us, inspire us, but do they convince us? Can we truly embrace these ideas; did our ancestors truly believe in such irrational and seemingly impossible things? The answer is yes, and no. Certainly some understood these accounts literally and found in them meaning and comfort, but they were likely few. Far more of our ancestors approached these teachings with caution or even distaste; as we might today, many urged their followers to interpret such descriptions figuratively, to see them only as metaphor.

But even as metaphor, these images hold tremendous power. They represent a world in which all is goodness, unity, abundance, and friendship. They represent a universe in which, our mystics taught, we find "the restoration of the original coexistence and correlation of all things."[9] They represent the Creation God gave us once—and has longed to entrust to us again.

And, after all, the promise of the natural world redeemed is just so irresistible. Not even the supremely rational Maimonides could remain unmoved: advising his readers not to expect that "anything of the natural course of the world will cease or that any innovation will be introduced into creation," still he anticipated such "an abundance of worldly goods" in the Messianic Age that famine and war would end forever.[10]

What Will People Be Like in the Messianic Age?

The radical changes the Messiah will bring to the natural world are well matched by the changes we ourselves are to experience. According to messianic tradition, redemption will transform not only the human condition, but even the human form.

And this transformation will prove dramatic. "The height of a [person] in the Messianic Age will be two hundred cubits," one sage claims. "A hundred cubits!" rejoins another.[11] Either way, our appearance will match our stature: "In the future time to come," promises the *Zohar*, "the Holy One, blessed be God, will render the bodies of the pious beautiful."[12] Nor will we be marred by illness: "Even the sick, the Holy One, blessed be God, will command the sun to heal [them]," one midrash narrates. "God will cause living waters to come out of Jerusalem, and with them God will

heal all those afflicted by a disease."[13] And the Talmud even goes
so far as to describe our accessories: "In the World to Come ... the
righteous sit with crowns on their heads, basking in the radiance
of the *Shechinah*."[14]

Echoing the abundant fertility of the natural world, some
messianists ascribed amazing birthing powers to humanity in the
time of the Messiah. One passage enumerates six activities we will
undertake in the Messianic Age; most are the relaxed and unde-
manding duties we might anticipate, like sitting, eating and drinking, and enjoying God's Presence. But we also find on the list
"be fruitful and multiply."[15] And it is perhaps no wonder that the
divine command to bear children still holds in the Messianic Age;
after all, one midrash states, every Israelite is destined to have six
hundred thousand offspring![16]

It might appear easy to dismiss these traditions. At first
glance they seem to have little function besides shocking us or
entertaining us. What significance could possibly exist in an
argument over whether we will stand one hundred or two hundred cubits high? Why were our mystics preoccupied with looking good? And what if we simply don't want to bear six hundred
thousand children?

It was in such a context that Maimonides counseled, "All the
similar things said about the Messiah are but allegories.... All these
things and their likes, no one can know how they will be until
they will be."[17] Rather than focusing on the details of our physical
bodies—or questioning the wisdom of ancestors who appeared to
do so—let us view these passages as allegories, then, and examine
what deeper lessons might lie within them.

Why, we might begin by asking, does appearance matter in
the time of the Messiah? Didn't our ancestors share our conviction that inner being should take precedence over outward attrac-
tiveness? Didn't they, like us, appreciate the spiritual aspects of
redemption: the opportunity to commune with God, the glimpse
into the divine plan for humanity, the sudden apprehension of
life's meaning and purpose?

Gratifyingly—and perhaps surprisingly—we find meaningful responses to these queries contained in our ancestors' teachings. For one hundred and two hundred cubits are not measurements our sages proposed randomly or selected simply to astonish. Rather, one hundred cubits is the traditional height of the walls of the ancient Temple in Jerusalem, and incredibly, two hundred cubits is the height legend assigns to the first human Adam, until he shrank after disobeying God by eating the fruit of the Tree of Knowledge. Invoking these numbers to describe our stature, then, our ancestors proclaim that the Messianic Age will raise us to a new level of goodness; we will merit comparison to the most sacred place in the world and return to a state of being unmarked by sin. Indeed, the *Zohar* expressly links the splendor of the righteous to "the beauty of Adam the first man when he entered the Garden of Eden."[18] Redeemed from evil—from the evil done to us by others, to be sure, but no less from our own capacity for wickedness—we are restored to the innocence and purity of Creation, to the time before wrongdoing, to the fullness and the glory God has intended for us all along. We are again worthy of basking in the radiance of God's Presence, of wearing the crown of the righteous.

And this redemption recalls an earlier redemption: our going forth from slavery in Egypt. One of the seminal events in our history as a people, the Exodus became for our ancestors a paradigm of God's saving power and a promise of future deliverance from all persecution and suffering. According to tradition, the number of Israelite slaves God redeemed from Egypt was six hundred thousand. In imagining that each woman would bear six hundred thousand children, then, our ancestors affirm that the messianic redemption will be truly complete; those who come into the world from now on will be like those rescued from Egypt—they will live in freedom and know the liberating might of the Divine.

What, then, will humanity be like in the days of the Messiah? Unless we wish to take literally our ancestors' descriptions—which they, most likely, intended as metaphor—we cannot answer with regard to our height, our appearance, or our activities. Rather, we must say with Maimonides, "No one can know how they will be until they will be." And yet we do know this: our souls will be pure, our spirits free, our beings sanctified—and our potential for goodness at last realized.

What Will Society Be Like in the Messianic Age?

No longer threatened by wild animals, the whims of nature, or the malice of humanity, we are truly free in the days of the Messiah. We can create the society we wish, build a collective life not according to our needs—after all, each of our needs, from protection to sustenance, is now satisfied in abundance!—but based solely upon our desires.

What shape might this new civilization take? After generations of deprivation, persecution, and want, for what did our ancestors yearn most? And what can we learn from their messianic visions and descriptions of the ideal society?

We might look for intricate and fanciful narratives. After their elaborate portrayals of the birth pangs of the Messiah—from sinister governments and riotous children to scorching famine and bloody combat—surely our ancestors would spin equally fantastic stories about a redeemed and triumphant society. Perhaps they would bring to vivid life a community awash in ecstasy or at least sampling the physical pleasures so long denied them: enjoying lavish meals, adorning themselves with perfume and fine clothing and precious jewels, soaking in warm baths, even engaging in some passionate lovemaking or imbibing a bit of good wine.

We might look for these depictions, but we would look in vain. Messianic literature evinces little interest in such extravagance. With every delight at last available, our ancestors would choose instead simplicity, and communion, and peace.

Maimonides gives magnificent voice to this truth in his view of life in the Messianic Age:

> The sages said that the only difference between this world and the days of the Messiah will be with regard to the

enslavement to the kingdoms. The sages and the prophets yearned for the days of the Messiah not in order that they should rule over the whole world, and not in order that they should lord it over the idolaters, and not in order that the nations should elevate them, and not in order that they should eat and drink and rejoice; but in order that they should devote themselves to the Torah and its wisdom, and that there be nobody to oppress them and to negate.[19]

There is no excess in this messianic society; once redeemed from her tormentors, Israel will have no interest in self-glorification or self-indulgence. Rather, we will cherish our freedom—not the freedom to do whatever we please, but the freedom to live untroubled and to spend our days in pursuit of holiness.

Even the more exuberant teachings echo Maimonides's convictions. One midrash exalts our grandeur in the Messianic Age, but rather than signifying superiority or power, this grandeur means only that we "will have no fear of any creature."[20] Another passage predicting that "there will be no single individual who will not possess land in mountain, lowland, and valley"[21] proves less striking in its portrait of wealth than in its remarkable call for equal distribution of property. And still another tradition envisages all people speaking Hebrew in the time of the Messiah—as an expression not of Israel's victory, however, but of the oneness of humanity: "In This World ... My creatures became divided into seventy languages," God muses. "But in the World to Come all will become equal, and shoulder to shoulder they will call upon My Name."[22]

It is beautiful—and poignant, and even plaintive—to see how little our ancestors would ask for themselves in the time of redemption. Even after so much hardship, they would not lose themselves in luxury; even after so much oppression, they would not lose themselves in vengeance; even after so much poverty, they would not lose themselves in acquisitiveness. Once redeemed, they wanted only a society founded on friendship and justice and equality and the love of God; and they wanted all of God's creatures—all the races and nations represented by the figurative "seventy languages"—to share in this messianic civilization.

According to Rabbinic literature, Moses shared with the freed Israelite slaves a vision of this world:

> You have seen all the miracles and great deeds and marvels which the Holy One, blessed be God, performed for you. Much more than that will God do for you in the Future to Come. For not like This World is the World to Come. In This World there are wars and sufferings and [human evil] ... and they have permission to rule the world. But in the World to Come there will be no sufferings, no hatred ... no sighs, no enslavement ... as it is written [in the Bible], "The Eternal God will wipe away the tears from all faces" [Isaiah 25:8].[23]

This is our ancestors' portrayal of society redeemed. A millennium and a half later, it may be ours as well.

When the Messiah Is Here, How Will Judaism Be Practiced?

When God first forged a covenant with Abraham and when our ancestors affirmed that covenant in the wilderness of Sinai, the Jewish people promised to follow God's ways and to fulfill God's will. We vowed to live out the words of Torah and to engage in God's commandments. In short, we committed ourselves to the practice of Judaism.

This commitment is eternal and unchanging. But *the way in which we practice* our Judaism is not unchanging at all. Examples are abundant: Hanukkah, one of Judaism's best-known holidays, is not mentioned in the Torah; it was, in fact, inspired by events that took place long after those the Bible describes. The thrice-daily prayer services that serve as a hallmark of traditional Judaism were not biblically mandated; rather, they replaced the thrice-daily animal sacrifices—our earliest method of worshipping God—after the destruction of the Second Temple in 70 CE. Prohibitions against

driving cars on Shabbat, eating cheeseburgers or chicken parme-
san, and submitting to autopsies that are not medically necessary
cannot be found in Judaism's original legal codes; they arose millennia later, as rabbis sought to apply the Torah's teachings to an
industrial age. And it is worth noting that while bagels, the long
black coats and black hats of Hasidic men, and even exchanging
gifts on Hanukkah have become staples of Jewish culture, each
originated in the non-Jewish world.

For thousands of years we have ensured Judaism's survival by
adapting our customs and celebrations to reflect historical circumstances and to respond to new realities. And messianic tradition
promises that this phenomenon will fully flower with the arrival of
the Messiah! The Jewish people will retain unique traditions—and
a unique relationship with God—but will express our Judaism very
differently in an era of redemption.

We will find the daily and yearly rhythms of Jewish life altered
completely. In an age of universal plenty and peace, our sages reasoned, we would no longer recite traditional blessings importun-
ing God for a bountiful crop, justice, or deliverance; nor, with
our potential for goodness at last fulfilled, would we petition God
for understanding, repentance, or forgiveness. What, then, will
remain? In the Messianic Age, the Talmud proclaims, "all prayers
will be abolished—except for the prayer of thanksgiving."[24] We
may not need to ask God for anything after we are redeemed, but
we will still be saying thank You!

And just as we will be asking less of God, God will be requiring
less of us. A midrash asserts, "All festivals will [when the Messiah
arrives] be abolished—except for Purim, which will never be abolished."[25] What is the significance of Purim? While Yom Kippur
and Passover are well-known for the restrictions they place upon
us,[26] they are not unique in making demands; indeed, almost every
biblical festival mandates an additional sacrifice (enacted today as
an additional prayer service) and orders us to refrain from work—
that is, from using electricity and money, writing and drawing and
building, and venturing beyond a prescribed distance from our

home. The sole exception is Purim, a day that enjoins us only to read and rejoice in a delightful (and relatively short!) story of Jewish triumph.[27] In the Messianic Age, then, our festival obligations appear to consist simply of happily recalling past episodes of salvation!

So powerful will our redemption be, in fact, that we will soon forget everything except this salvation. Even the bitterness of four hundred years as slaves in Egypt will fade in the face of our messianic deliverance, one text foretells.[28] And the Hebrew month of Av—traditionally a time for fasting, reading lamentations, and bewailing the lost Temples in Jerusalem—will in the Messianic Age turn to jubilation. "In the month of Av, during which they mourned [the Messiah ben Joseph] and in which Jerusalem was destroyed, there will be great joy for Israel," *Sefer Zerubbabel* promises.[29] No doubt reflecting this theme, some medieval Eastern European Jews who believed the Messiah was soon to appear permitted their children to spend Tisha b'Av—the fifteenth of Av, and the anniversary of the Temples' destruction—running wild,[30] and Shabbatei Zevi's seventeenth-century followers observed the day with ecstatic celebration.

Perhaps the most dramatic of these changes, however, is expressed by the prophet Jeremiah and later mystical literature: not only prayers, holidays, and history but also the word of God as we know it will be left behind. Delivered from our own intellectual, moral, and spiritual shortcomings, we are at last able to communicate with God clearly and purely, and this clarity and purity transcend even the holy Torah.[31] Rather than retaining a covenant whose laws we have so often violated, God will enter into a completely new covenant with redeemed Israel; and rather than seeking God's law from external sources, we will look inside ourselves to discover the Divine.

In the stirring words of Jeremiah:

See, a new time is coming, declares the Eternal, when I will make a new covenant with the House of Israel and the

House of Judah. It will not be like the covenant I made with their ancestors when I took them by the hand to lead them out of Egypt, a covenant which they broke.... But such is the covenant I will make with the House of Israel after these days, declares the Eternal: I will put My Torah into their inmost being, and inscribe it upon their hearts (Jeremiah 31:31–33).

And an obscure Yemenite midrash engagingly envisions this new revelation:

> The Messiah will sit in the Yeshiva [the house of study], and all those who walk on earth will come and sit before him to hear a new Torah and new commandments and the deep wisdom. And no person who hears a teaching from the mouth of the Messiah will ever forget it, for the Holy One, blessed be God, will reveal the Divine Presence in the House of Study of the Messiah, and will pour the Divine Spirit into all who walk on earth, and the Divine Spirit will be upon each and every one. And all will understand Jewish law on their own, the midrash on their own, the commentaries on their own, the legends on their own, the traditions on their own ... and all will have their own House of Study, the House of the Divine Presence.[32]

These changes are striking, challenging, fascinating—but what do they signify? Most obviously, they reflect the joy of redemption and the expansive sense that we are at last free to enjoy our lives fully. But more importantly, they also establish that *we* are somehow different, and better. Having fulfilled the divine promise God implanted within us, we are finally able to practice—and to understand—Judaism in a different and better way. Less inclined to sin, we require fewer commandments; and more attuned to God's presence and God's power, we can focus not on the minutiae of law and ritual, but on the deepest and most meaningful aspects of our relationship with the Eternal.

What Is the Resurrection of the Dead?

According to the famous words of Benjamin Franklin, "In this world nothing is certain but death and taxes." In the world redeemed—the world of the Messiah—we would not expect to find taxes, and neither do we find death!

The book of Isaiah puts it beautifully: in the Time to Come, promises the prophet, God "will destroy death forever. My Eternal God will wipe away the tears from all faces" (Isaiah 25:8). It is a glorious image—mourning replaced by comfort, loss replaced by enduring life. And it is only the beginning: Not only will people cease to die in the age of redemption, messianic tradition asserts, but those who have already passed away shall return.

While we may associate such teachings with Christianity, this tenet—*Techiat haMetim* in Hebrew, translated literally as "the resurrection of the dead"—actually holds a central place in Jewish faith. Throughout the Talmud and midrash we find visions of a world filled with revitalized bodies and restored souls. "Because You renew our spirits each and every morning [as we awaken]," one sage reasoned, "we are certain that in Your great faithfulness You will [return] our spirits to us at the resurrection."[33] And, anticipating the resurrection of the dead, a rabbi with his last breaths enjoined his disciples, "Dress me in white raiment with borders, put socks on my legs, sandals on my feet, and a staff in my hand. Lay me on my side near the road, so that when the Messiah comes, I will be ready!"[34] Later generations maintained—and amplified—such beliefs; Moses Maimonides even counted the resurrection of the dead among Judaism's thirteen essential principles.

This principle, however, is significantly more controversial than, say, the oneness of God. The Bible provides no explicit promise or practical explanation of the resurrection of the dead, forcing our sages to root their convictions in cryptic and fleeting scriptural allusions. Uncomfortably, aspects of the resurrection also appeared to reflect the influence of pagan culture and to parallel the theology of an emerging Christianity.[35] And in modern times, many Jews have deemphasized or even discarded the concept, dismissing it as unenlightened and irrational.

A closer examination may explain why the resurrection of the dead is not universally embraced. The event is not allegorical nor figurative; bodies are literally to be revived, be reunited with the appropriate soul, rise from the earth, and return to life. Because the resurrection will take place in Israel, those Jews buried in the Holy Land will emerge with ease; others, according to tradition, will tunnel underground until they reach Jerusalem. (While the midrash assures us that God will make passages[36] for the righteous, the less pious will presumably have a lot of digging to do!) Finally, God will bring forth Abraham and Sarah, raising them last in order that they might behold the spectacular fulfillment of God's ancient promise: to make their descendants as numerous as the stars of heaven and the sand on the shores of the sea.[37]

While our ancestors were not unaware of the problems posed by the resurrection of the dead, they proved remarkably resilient in working out the details. Will we, for example, appear naked or clothed? Clothed, one sage explained: "If the wheat, which is buried [that is, planted] naked [that is, as an unadorned seed] rises in several garments [that is, layers], how much more so the pious who are buried in their clothes!"[38] If we are blind, deaf, or disfigured in life, will our resurrected bodies bear the same affliction? Not for long, we are assured; we will come up from the ground in the same form in which we lived, just so that we will recognize one another, but immediately afterward, God will cure us. What if a person has been dismembered, burned, or consumed? Ideally, God will rebuild our bodies from the bone at the back of the neck upon which the knot of the tefillin rests, but if that is not possible, God will completely re-create us. How will everyone fit in the Land of Israel? The tenth-century sage Saadia Gaon holds there will be plenty of room.[39] And finally, what of a widower who had remarried—with which spouse would he be reunited? Such questions, our Rabbis demurred, would be answered at the time of the resurrection—by history's most eminent, and conveniently revived, prophets.

But the influence of the resurrection of the dead is hardly limited to fervent believers and their theoretical discussions. In its teachings we find also the origin of mainstream Jewish funeral practices, like burying a body facing east (toward Jerusalem), including in the grave a handful of soil from the Holy Land, or placing in the coffin items stained with the blood of the deceased.[40] And, perhaps unknowingly, Jews declare faith in the resurrection every time they recite the traditional *Amidah,* for in the second blessing, the blessing extolling God's might, are found these words: "Who is like You, Mighty One, and who can compare to You? For You are the Sovereign who kills and who resurrects.... It is certain that You will resurrect the dead. You are blessed, Eternal One, Resurrector of the dead."[41] Even the prayer's praise of God for "keep[ing] faith with those who sleep in the dust" contains a reference to the resurrection; although "those who sleep in the dust" are often envisioned as the homeless or needy, they are actually the dead, loyally waiting to be restored.

Reared in a milieu that prizes rationality, empiricism, and logical thinking, we may shrink from this aspect of our heritage. And yet surely even the most astute and enlightened can at least appreciate what is represented by the resurrection of the dead. It is, first, a testament to the importance of this world and of our corporeal selves. This life, these bodies, are not profane shells to be transcended or sloughed off; rather, they are vestures of glory, divine handiwork, and worthy of redemption.[42] The resurrection of the dead also proclaims the unmatched power of God and the control God exerts over even the most basic laws of nature.

And finally, with the destruction of death, the resurrection affirms the triumph of life.

What Is the Feast of the Righteous?

Even the pious need to let loose once in a while. Or, to be more specific, once.

Amid rhapsodic descriptions of the serene, just, and peaceful life that awaits in the Messianic Age, we find spirited accounts of what promises to be a truly once-in-an-eternity experience. This event—extremely exclusive and occurring for one day only—features dishes never before sampled, meticulously aged wine, and the finest entertainment ever arranged. It is the Feast of the Righteous.

While our sages indeed prized modesty and virtue over indulgence and frivolity in the age of redemption, still they anticipated a little fun. And thankfully so! Their depictions of the marvelous Feast of the Righteous are completely original—neither the Torah nor our prophets foretell such an occasion—and wonderfully illuminate our ancestors' understanding of mythic beasts, the enduring significance of biblical leaders, and even the nature of divine power. Plus, the tales are absolutely a delight to read!

As its name implies, the Feast of the Righteous includes only the most pious of Israel. Greeted by archangels Michael and Gabriel[43] and "accompanied by the *Shechinah* [Divine Presence] with a myriad myriads of ministering angels, with pillars of lightning round about them, and sparks of splendor [surrounding] them, and fireworks of radiance [making] their faces glow, and sparks of light [making] their eyelids shine,"[44] guests will gather at a table set by God in the Garden of Eden. There they are arrayed "in royal robes, and with a royal crown, and with jewels of kingly pearls, [a]nd each one sits like a [sovereign] upon [a] royal throne." Outside Eden's gates lurk the wicked, who "stretch their height to one hundred cubits so as to be able to see the honor of the pious"—and, beholding the reception granted the righteous, are immediately moved to repentant praise of God.

Among those entering Eden are history's most exalted: the first man Adam and his son Seth; the patriarchs Abraham, Isaac, and Jacob; famed monarchs Saul, David, Solomon, and Hezekiah; and of course Moses, Elijah, and the Messiah. But this is not all, and it is easy to picture our sages' excitement as they composed what follows: "Is there a host who makes a banquet for the guests," the assembled chide their benefactor, "but does not sit down with them?"[45] And so an acquiescent God joins the proceedings, serving

food and drink and even leading the sun, moon, and stars in dancing to music played by the ministering angels.[46]

But there is still more to come. The menu, in fact, proves
particularly evocative. The drink of choice, the midrash relates,
is "wine preserved in its grapes since the six days of Creation."[47]
Whether we understand this wine literally or figuratively—most
sources depict the guests as consuming actual wine, but the *Zohar*
interprets "drinking wine" as an allegorical reference to receiving
esoteric knowledge of God so far withheld from humanity—the
significance remains the same: just as redemption has been part of
God's plan from the beginning, so too has this magnificent prize
for the pious. From the world's earliest moments and even—or,
perhaps, especially—through the darkest periods of Jewish life,
God has intended to reward those who fulfilled the divine will—
and kept believing in the divine promise.

Of course, not even the finest wine can be served without food!
Before our vegetarian diet takes hold, the righteous are permitted
one more meal of meat—and what a meal it is! Three selections
are offered, each for the first and last time in history: Leviathan,
the legendary sea monster invoked most strikingly in the books
of Isaiah and Job; Behemoth, the brute of the mountains; and
mighty Ziz, the fierce, saber-clawed great bird. How these creatures will end up on the plates of the righteous is a subject of
playful dispute. According to one tradition, the female Leviathan
and Behemoth have been long preserved by God for exactly this
occasion;[48] another holds that the prophet Jonah will arise and
slay Leviathan, fulfilling a vow he made to God while still in the
belly of the fish;[49] and yet another contends that Israel will kill
Behemoth, Ziz will maul Leviathan to death, and Moses will come
to slaughter Ziz.[50] And lest we wonder how our pious ancestors
allowed themselves to indulge in the nonkosher meat of these
beasts, God reassures us in a midrash, "An exceptional temporary
ruling [permitting the consumption] will go forth from Me."[51]

Again, such wild passages hold deeper meaning. Although
these monsters are not important figures in Jewish lore—indeed,

they likely originated in pagan Near Eastern cultures and merit only fleeting mention in the Bible—they fit perfectly into our ancestors' conceptions of the Feast of the Righteous. The mythical animals represented the enemies of Israel, to be sure, but even more important, they symbolized chaos, disorder, darkness, and turmoil. Many ancient tales of creation—including our own, preserved in the opening chapter of the book of Genesis—envision creation as a triumphant act, a divine being's imposition of order upon the forces of chaos and evil. Slaughtering and consuming Leviathan, Behemoth, and Ziz, then, would be a reenactment of the Creation story—and a reestablishment of divine order in the underwater, earthly, and heavenly realms.

And perhaps it was this order that gladdened our ancestors most of all. Compared with the debauchery of the Persian king Ahasuerus's banquet in the biblical book of Esther or accounts of the parties in which the Romans indulged during the time of the Talmudic sages, the Feast of the Righteous appears tame, innocent, even sweet. After all, how can things possibly veer out of control when Moses and the Messiah are seated at the table? How can the entertainment devolve into lewdness when God is leading the dancing? And how can guests become gluttonous when the meal begins with a proper *berachah* (blessing), recited by King David, no less?[52] For all of the extravagance our ancestors anticipated, they wanted festivities steeped in Jewish values, a gathering that God and the heroes of old would be proud to attend. The Feast of the Righteous was not a departure from, but a celebration of, God's law and the divine order.

And this table of the pious would be only the beginning. Delivered and transformed, our entire world would at last be ready to welcome God's glorious rule. For redemption not only would render the universe the dwelling place of the Messiah but would inaugurate the dominion of the true Savior, the Holy One, blessed be God.

CHAPTER FIVE

The Messiah Will Establish God's Dominion

In the first years of the Common Era a messianist recorded this vision:

> And then God's dominion shall appear throughout all
>   the divine creation,
> And then evil shall be no more, and sorrow shall
>   depart with it ...
> For the Most High will arise, the Eternal God alone ...
> And you shall give thanks and acclaim your
>   Creator.[1]

It is among the most magnificent depictions of the Messianic Age in pseudepigraphic literature, but something essential appears to be missing. At the climax of redemption, when the battles have been fought and the necessary transformations achieved, only "the Most High will arise, the Eternal God *alone*."[2] Where is the instrument of this redemption; where is the Messiah? He is nowhere to be found.

Nor does this text prove an aberration. As our messianic hopes near realization, we see time and again the figure of the

Messiah deemphasized, diminished, and finally disappearing. For the Messiah's work is done; all that remains is for our Savior to arise and to inaugurate divine rule over a redeemed universe.

And there can be no place for the Messiah here. Judaism is clear and unambiguous on this point: for all of the Messiah's singular qualities and mighty acts, he does not share in the divinity of God and, like all of God's creations, must yield his place—and his glory—before the Most High.[3] Some traditions explicitly underscore this conviction by teaching that the process of redemption encompasses two distinct eras: while deliverance will begin to unfold in *Yamot HaMashiach*, the days of the Messiah, its most celebrated promises will be fulfilled only by God, and only after the Messiah has come—and gone—in *Olam Haba*, the World to Come.[4]

These, then, are the Messiah's final and perhaps most wondrous tasks: After leading his people to triumph and salvation, the Messiah steps aside to reveal a Sovereign far greater than he. And having brought the world as close as he might to an age of absolute justice and perfect peace, the Messiah fades away—that God might complete the work and make at last this universe a worthy dwelling place of the Divine Presence.

Who Is Elijah?

We first encounter the prophet Elijah in the biblical book of Kings.[5] The time is the ninth century BCE, the place the northern kingdom of Israel, and the situation a religious crisis. Israel's ruler King Ahab has betrayed his people and his God, wedding the infamous idol-worshipper Jezebel, establishing a shrine to the pagan deity Ba'al, and remaining silent as Jezebel slaughters hundreds of Israelite prophets. After years of hiding, Elijah returns to unify the Israelites against foreign gods and destroy the followers of Ba'al who had led them astray; although Jezebel's vengefulness soon forces Elijah underground again, he eventually emerges to confront Ahab and compel the king to humble himself before the Eternal.

Elijah's deeds are staggering, his zeal for God awesome. But perhaps even more amazing than his acts in this world is Elijah's departure from it. Accompanied by his loyal disciple Elisha, Elijah parts the Jordan River with his mantle, allowing the two men to cross on dry land. On the other side, the Bible relates,

> a fiery chariot with fiery horses suddenly appeared and separated one from the other; and Elijah went up to heaven in a whirlwind. Elisha saw it, and he cried out, "Oh, father, father! Israel's chariots and horsemen!" When he could no longer see them, he grasped his garments and rent them in two. (2 Kings 2:11–12)[6]

It is likely this combination of passionate life and not-quite-death that rendered Elijah the focus of the messianic—and Jewish— imagination. Taken alive to heaven, Jewish tradition teaches, Elijah serves as Israel's quasi-ambassador to God, interceding on our behalf and promoting our interests before the celestial throne. He also makes periodic visits to earth, advising the great sages of the generation and bestowing wealth on the pious and needy of Israel.[7] Wonderful legends describe his devotion. In many folktales, he disguises himself as a beggar, then rewards with riches those who show him hospitality. In one story, he consoles a rabbi bewildered by the apparent injustice of this world, "You may see something that you cannot make sense of—a wicked person seems to be rewarded or a righteous person suffers. Know that these things are not always as they seem. Trust God and keep your faith."[8] And in a particularly poignant passage, he takes up before God the case of sinful parents seeking to be reunited with their innocent children in the Messianic Age. "Master of the World!" Elijah intones. "Which is the greater divine attribute—the attribute of goodness or the attribute of chastisement? Surely the attribute of goodness is ample, and the attribute of chastisement is scant!" And the Eternal, as always, responds to Elijah's words: "Well did you plead their ... defense," God concedes. "Let [the parents] come to [their children]."[9]

And what better way for Elijah to demonstrate his love for Israel than heralding the time of redemption? The connection of Elijah to our salvation is nearly three thousand years old. The prophet Malachi was the first to link the two, foretelling that God "will send the prophet Elijah to you before the coming of the great and terrible Day of the Eternal! He shall reconcile parents with children and children with parents, so that ... I do not strike the whole land with utter destruction" (Malachi 3:23–24). By the first century, Elijah had been embraced as the Messiah's forerunner in virtually all Jewish circles, and while many Rabbinic sages—fearful that the fervor with which some fringe groups regarded Elijah would spread to mainstream Judaism—downplayed his significance, the designation persisted. From Talmudic to apocalyptic to medieval to modern texts, we find stirring passages like this one:

> At the time the Holy One redeems Israel, three days before the Messiah comes, [the prophet] Elijah will come and stand upon the mountains of Israel and weep and lament over them, and then will say: "O mountains of Israel, how long will you continue to be wasteland, dry and desolate?" Elijah's voice will be heard from world's end to world's end. But then he will say to the mountains of Israel: "Peace has come to the world." On the second day, Elijah will come and stand upon the mountains of Israel, and say: "Good has come to the world." And on the third day, he will come and say: "Salvation has come to the world."[10]

Even familiar and not overtly messianic rituals echo this theme: the door is opened for Elijah at every Passover Seder; he is praised as the bringer of good tidings to Israel in the traditional *Birkat HaMazon,* or Grace after Meals; and immediately after ending Shabbat with the *Havdalah*[11] service, Jews implore Elijah to bring the Messiah "speedily and in our day."

Many texts envision Elijah not only as the announcer of the Messiah, but as an active participant in the drama of redemption.

Some attest to Elijah's role as a warrior for God and the Messiah, numbering him among the traditional "four world conquerors"[12] and praising him as "destined to overthrow the foundations of the heathen."[13] Yet far more accounts invoke Elijah as a healer. Whether settling disputes over the intricacies of religious law or bringing those wrongly excluded back to the Jewish community, Elijah will reconcile all Israel with one another—and in doing so, messianic tradition promises, "make peace in the world."[14] And Elijah will ensure that this peace is real and everlasting: it shall be he, our sages taught, who oversees the resurrection of the dead[15] and who carries the precious flask of oil that formally anoints the Messiah.[16]

And, of course, it shall be Elijah who declares that the dominion of God has at last arisen. For immediately after he declares on the third day, "Salvation has come to the world," does redemption truly begin. "In that hour," the midrash relates, "the Holy One will show the divine glory and the divine sovereignty to all the inhabitants of the [universe]."[17]

What Is the Role of the Shofar?

Like the prophet and herald Elijah, the shofar finds its origins in the Bible and its climax in the Messianic Age.

In the chilling story of the *Akedah*—the Binding of Isaac, recorded in Genesis 22:1–19—our patriarch Abraham comes horribly close to offering his son as a sacrifice to God. Only when the slaughtering knife has been raised to young Isaac's throat does an angel reveal that the entire ordeal has been a test to verify Abraham's fealty to the Eternal. "And when Abraham looked up, his eye fell upon a ram, caught in the thicket by its horns," the Torah relates. "So Abraham went and took the ram and offered it up as a burnt offering in place of his son" (Genesis 22:13).

But this proves no ordinary ram—and no ordinary sacrifice. The ram's horns are not consumed nor discarded; rather, "not one thing went to waste," Jewish legend marvels. "Of his two horns, the one was blown at the revelation [of Torah] at Mount Sinai, and the other will be used to proclaim the end of the Exile."[18]

Beautiful—although contradictory—texts illustrate exactly how this shofar will announce our salvation. According to one tradition, the archangel Michael will blow the shofar in order to summon Elijah and the Messiah for the apocalyptic war against Armilus, "and all Israel will know the sound of the shofar, and will hear that [God] has redeemed Israel."[19] Most teachings, however, envisage Elijah as the keeper of the exalted horn; some even calculate how many times he will sound the shofar and what will happen each time he does. One pseudepigraphic passage narrates:

> The Messiah will command Elijah to blow the shofar, and the light of the moon will be like the light of the sun, and God will send full healing to all the sick.... The second blast which Elijah will blow will make the dead rise ... and all will come to the Messiah from the four corners of the earth, from east and from west, from north and from south.... And at the third blast which he shall blow, will appear the *Shechinah*, the Divine Presence of God.[20]

The picture of all Israel heeding the call of the shofar and gathering "from east and from west, from north and from south" proves particularly evocative. In the *Amidah* prayer, Jews entreat God to "sound the great shofar for our freedom, and raise the banner to gather in our exiled people, and gather us together from the four corners of the earth." And this messianic image came to brief and vivid life in June 1967, just after the Six-Day War, when the chief rabbi of the Israeli army sounded the shofar at the liberated Western Wall.

In between these events, however—the *Akedah* and the redemption—stretch thousands of years. And we know well that the shofar serves essential functions in these intervening eras; while the shofar of the ram slaughtered by Abraham may be stored up for the day of deliverance, every generation has ritually prepared their own ram's horns and sounded their own *shofarot*.[21] Used for musical, ceremonial, and practical purposes, the shofar became one of the most useful tools—as well as one of the most compelling symbols—in Jewish history.

Today, of course, we associate the shofar primarily with the High Holy Days. At the climax of the Rosh Hashanah morning service, the shofar calls us to "awake, you sleepers, from your sleep! Rouse yourselves, you slumberers, out of your slumber. Examine your deeds, and turn to God in repentance. Remember your Creator!"[22] In a series of dramatic readings and blasts, we acclaim God's sovereignty, invoke God's infinite memory of time long past, and praise the divine revelation. And nine days later, the great and awesome Yom Kippur—the Day of Atonement—concludes with a single blow of the shofar: a triumphant *tekiah gedolah* ringing out loud and long.

We might be surprised—and moved—to learn the additional and profound significance our annual sounding of the shofar truly holds. It hearkens back thousands of years to the *Akedah*—and forward hopefully not so many years to the day God will proclaim "the end of our Exile." For the shofar that we blow on Rosh Hashanah is intended first to remind God of the unquestioning faith Abraham and Isaac displayed during the *Akedah* and to exhort God to regard us, their children, with compassion. As God instructed after Abraham had sacrificed the ram in place of his son, "Your children will sin before Me in time to come, and I will sit in judgment upon them on Rosh Hashanah. If they desire that I should grant them pardon, they shall blow the shofar on that day, and I ... will forgive them for their sins."[23] For the sake of our ancestors, then, God will look upon us with mercy during the High Holy Days, overlooking transgressions that might otherwise deserve punishment; all that is required of us is that we sound the shofar. (But just in case God needed an extra reminder, our sages mandated as the Torah portion for Rosh Hashanah morning the story of the *Akedah*!)

But even more than looking back, the call of the shofar urges history forward. For in sounding the shofar in Rosh Hashanah, we do not only observe that year's holy day; we also anticipate the blasts that will echo across God's creation to announce that redemption has arrived at last. The "shofar-sound heralds another day, whose promise is our hope," the liturgy of the Reform Rosh Hashanah shofar service reads. "Then shall begin the time of peace of which we dream; a world of truth shall be revealed to us; and together we shall rejoice in the dominion of God."[24]

As we celebrate the birth of the world on Rosh Hashanah, then, so do we look toward its culmination: a time when the blast we hear in the synagogue will echo across the world, and when the shofar that sounds will be the one Abraham grasped so long ago, the one destined to "proclaim the end of the Exile" and call forth the *Shechinah*, the Divine Presence of God.

Will the Wicked Be Brought to Justice in the Messianic Age?

The joy of the Messianic Age is undeniable and abundant; but it is not—at least not yet—universal. Even in these heady days of redemption, Judaism retains its central tenets of justice and righteousness, its promise that goodness will be rewarded and wickedness punished. And so salvation will feel quite different for those who kept God's law and for those who cast it aside.

For the days of the Messiah are to be not only an era of triumph and glory, gladness and peace, they are to be, perhaps foremost, an age of justice. "Our Justice" even stands among the names our sages gave the Messiah,[25] and in marvelous—and occasionally terrifying—images, our ancestors anticipated the divine judgment and perfect justice that would come in his wake.

This aspect of the Messianic Age likely originated with our biblical prophets. Passionately calling for judgment and justice, they remind us that righteousness stands as an essential component of Israel's redemption. "Listen to this, you who devour the needy, annihilating the poor of the land ... using an ephah that is too small, and a shekel that is too big [that is, giving less but charging more], tilting a dishonest scale, and selling grain refuse as grain!" Amos castigated his people in God's name, before concluding darkly, "The Eternal swears by the Pride of Jacob: 'I will never forget any of their doings'" (Amos 8:4–7). Even more chillingly, the prophet Malachi warns:

> You shall come to see the difference between one who
> has served the Eternal and one who has not.... The day
> is at hand, burning like an oven. All the arrogant and all
> the doers of evil shall be straw, and the day that is com-
> ing—said the Eternal of Hosts—shall burn them to ashes.
> (Malachi 3:18–19)

How—and if—judgment would truly be passed on the wicked
of Israel in the time of deliverance, however, remains unclear.
Although Jewish teachings hold that we will indeed be called to
account for our wrongdoings in this world, many sources envisage
this judgment taking place immediately after death; by the time
the Messiah arrives, then, most souls will have already received
their just rewards—and retributions. Therefore, messianic tradition generally concerns itself not with the fate of each person[26]
but with the people as a whole; and certainly the collective nation
of Israel had already been punished for—and forgiven of—her
sins during the dreadful *chevlei Mashiach,* the birth pangs of the
Messiah. Even those texts that do foresee a messianic judgment
for Israel often employ a benevolent, loving tone; one offers a
humorous parable to explain how God judges the body and soul
together,[27] another depicts the archangels Michael and Gabriel
washing repentant sinners and clothing them in "beautiful and
good garments,"[28] and a particularly tender passage exhorts Israel
not to fear God's verdict because "God is one of your city, one of
your relatives ... and most of all, God is your Parent."[29]

Rather, as post-prophetic tradition enthusiastically amplified,
God's judgment in the Messianic Age would fall heavy and dreadful not on Israel, but on those who had afflicted her.[30] Some of
our ancestors anticipated a specific Day of Judgment, at which the
biblical books of Joel and Daniel appear to hint, during which the
nations of the world would assemble in the Valley of Jehoshaphat
to hear the divine verdict pronounced upon them. And the news
would not be good: "In those days, when I restore the fortunes of
Judah and Jerusalem," God tells Israel's tormentors, "I will gather
all the nations and ... I will contend with them over My very own

people Israel, whom they scattered.... I will sit in judgment over all the nations ... for great is their iniquity" (Joel 4:1–2, 4:12–13). God will command them to walk across a bridge over Gehenna, a Jewish equivalent of hell, a midrashic text relates, "but as they reach the middle, the bridge will seem to have shrunk to the thinness of a thread, and they will fall."[31] Intones the pseudepigraphic *1 Enoch*: "God will deliver them for punishment, to execute vengeance on them, for they have oppressed God's children and God's elect. The wrath of the Lord of Spirits shall rest upon them, and God's sword shall be drunk with their blood."[32] But these sufferings are deserved, the midrash assures, and the wicked should not dispute their fate; even the stricken in Gehenna, one passage tells, utter the words, "Thou hast spoken rightly; Thou hast judged rightly."[33]

Although we find an undeniable—and discomfiting—element of vengefulness in these images, we may also be struck by our tradition's unwavering commitment to absolute justice. While it would be temptingly easy to abandon the painful memories of Jewish suffering and focus solely on the joys promised in the Messianic Age, our ancestors understood the importance of recalling, acknowledging—and yes, even avenging—the terrible wrongs that had been perpetrated upon our people. Although redemption was now at hand, what had come before still mattered; the deaths of our martyrs, the anguish of our ancestors, could not be forgotten. Justice would not be sacrificed in the name of salvation; indeed, only through justice could God truly and fully redeem the world.

But the judgment and justice of the Messianic Age do not end with recompense and chastisement. After God's justice has been rendered, and reward and punishment dispensed, there is, again and always, the opportunity for repentance. When the Day of Judgment has ended, one text soothes, the angel Gabriel will call upon God to bring forth those condemned to Gehenna that they might behold the glory of Israel. Genuinely moved to praise and friendship, they proclaim, "How beautiful is the Eternal! How beautiful God's beloved people!"[34] And in this moment the nations of the world are granted atonement and absolution; with these words they come to join Israel in a universal reconciliation—and a universal redemption.

Will Everyone Be Jewish in the Days of the Messiah?

According to messianic tradition, the answer to this question is simple and straightforward: yes. But how will the world come to embrace Judaism, and why—in an endless era of universal friendship and peace—will it even matter? Those are more complex, and perhaps even more intriguing, questions.

Since biblical times our ancestors have anticipated that in an age of redemption, humanity will accept God and acknowledge Judaism's truth.[35] As the prophet Micah exults:

> In the days to come, the Mount of the Eternal's House shall stand firm above the mountains, and it shall tower above the hills. The peoples shall gaze on it with joy, and the many nations shall go and shall say: "Come, let us go up to the Mount of the Eternal, to the House of the God of Jacob, that God may instruct us in the divine ways, and that we may walk in God's paths." (Micah 4:1–2)

And Zephaniah promises in God's name: "I will make the peoples pure of [that is, united in] speech, so that they all invoke the Eternal by name and serve God with one accord" (Zephaniah 3:9).

Later traditions echoed—and amplified—the convictions of our prophets. "All the nations and dominions will be assembled in one place: Jerusalem," a midrash unequivocally declares.[36] Another text envisages all of God's creatures standing together, "and shoulder to shoulder they will call upon My Name and will serve Me."[37] In a fascinating image, the *Zohar* relates that the light shining upon other nations will gradually fade away; this light will instead come to shine upon Israel and cause the "spirit of uncleanliness" at last to "pass from the world."[38]

While we might interpret these passages figuratively, some of our ancestors sought in them practical applications to their own

messianic expectations. No less an esteemed figure than Moses ben
Nachman, or Nachmanides—who eloquently defended Judaism in
a famed medieval disputation—envisioned our redeemer's coming before the pope and persuading him to accept the legitimacy
of the Jewish Messiah.[39] Similarly, medieval mystics—believing
that every generation possessed a potential savior—taught that the
Messiah would receive an audience with the pope and perhaps
even "[reveal] to him a bit of [esoteric] wisdom" in order to convince the papacy to "recognize the true religion."[40]

At first glance, our ancestors' insistence that all of humanity will "recognize the true religion" might appear small-minded,
even petty. But we likely feel our sympathy awakened as we consider the milieu in which our ancestors found themselves. Since
the rise of Christianity they had seen their messianic beliefs—
indeed, all of the beliefs they held dearest—at best undermined
and at worst made grounds for persecution and slaughter. Among
their few consolations, they clung to the idea that one day—the
day of deliverance—they would enjoy triumph and vindication
over their ridiculers and oppressors. And their concern about the
reaction of the gentile world also underscores a poignant sense
of vulnerability: after so many generations of being told they were
wrong about God, about how to serve the Eternal, and about the
nature and end of the world as they understood it, some of our
ancestors likely craved the approval—or at least the validation—of
those in power over them. While messianic tradition was willing
to extend the blessings of redemption to the entire world, our
ancestors first needed at least an acknowledgment that we had
been right all along.

But, of course, that is not the whole story. While emotion may
have played a role in the pervasiveness and longevity of this tenet,
a much higher—and more universal—impulse inspired and sustained it. For our ancestors truly, fully, and passionately believed in
the supremacy of Judaism, that only through the Torah could one
come to apprehend God and live with meaning and joyful purpose.
In imagining all of humanity "recogniz[ing] the true religion," then,

our ancestors asserted that the messianic redemption was to be a universal redemption; they welcomed even their most stiff-necked foes to realize what they had been missing—and finally to experience wholeheartedly the splendor of Jewish life. "Hearken to Me, O peoples, and give ear to Me, O nations!" Isaiah prophesies to the world in the name of God. "Teaching shall go forth from Me, My way for the light of peoples…. The triumph I grant is near…. My arms shall provide for the peoples" (Isaiah 51:4–5).[41]

In bringing the gentile nations into the fold of Judaism, then Israel would invite them to share in the magnificence of the Messianic Age, and in taking them under the wings of the Divine Presence, Israel would enable them finally to learn the glory of the Eternal. As one scholar notes:

> All should recognize the Eternal as the universal God … [for] in God alone can the nations of the earth find the salvation they so desperately need, desire, and seek. When they turn to the Eternal they shall be saved. And God's salvation will reach to the ends of the earth.[42]

How Will We Relate to God in the Messianic Age?

Some of our ancestors yearned to commune with God through the sacrifices commanded by the Torah. Others hoped to reach a new understanding of or even unity with the Divine, to feel at one with the world and its Creator.

And each anticipated that the age of redemption would fulfill these exalted expectations.

In traditional messianic thought, the rebuilding of the ancient Temple in Jerusalem—and the reestablishment of the sacrificial cult—held paramount importance. While we might shudder at the thought of ritually slaughtering animals in order to relate to the Divine, such was the system mandated by the Torah, and such was understood as the primary, most meaningful way of serving the Eternal. From the erection of the First Temple in Jerusalem until its destruction at the hands of Babylonia in 586 BCE, our forebears communicated with God—offering apologies, thanksgiving, or holy day observance—through sacrifices of livestock, birds, and choice flour.

With the fall of the First Temple, however, all that ended. And we may see the end of sacrifices as a necessary and welcome development in our religious life, but traditional Judaism viewed it quite differently. Although the sacrificial cult was revived during the Second Temple years—and although thrice-daily worship services later took the place of animal sacrifices—still our ancestors longed for the original and glorious Temple and to experience the divinely ordained way their own ancestors had related to God.

Even those among us who harbor no desire to return to an era of animal sacrifices may find ourselves moved by our ancestors' portrayals of the event. Taking heart from prophetic assurances that in the time of deliverance God's "sanctuary [would] abide among [Israel] forever" (Ezekiel 37:28),[43] they glowingly invoked the beauty of the Temple standing once again. One text proclaims:

> In Jerusalem there will be in the future, three thousand towers, each tower with seven thousand stories ... and the Temple will be on top of it all.... It will be built ... of purified gold, of clear gold, of drawn gold, and of Parwayim gold, which last one is like gold that produces fruit. And it will be set in sapphires and capped in greatness. Its height will reach heaven and until the stars ... and the Divine Presence of God will fill it.[44]

The breathless hyperbole does not mean our sages viewed the reestablishment of the Temple strictly as allegory—indeed, many anticipated an actual building, with actual priests wearing the garments detailed in the Torah presiding over actual sacrifices of actual animals[45]—but it does hint that our ancestors did not believe the Temple would serve as an end in itself. Rather, the vastness and the majesty of the reborn Temple would enable Israel to "reach heaven and until the stars"—that is, to approach God and commune closely and completely with the Divine. Not the building nor the sacrifices that would take place within it, but the connection with God that, our ancestors believed, would be forged and nourished remained the true object of longing.

While this restoration maintains a central place in messianic tradition, it is not the only means by which our ancestors hoped to relate to God during the days of salvation. In particular, the rational philosophers of the Middle Ages—who applied the principles of secular philosophy to the tenets of Jewish wisdom, and who are best exemplified by the venerated Moses Maimonides— looked forward also to an era of uninterrupted contemplation of God's nature and essence. For them, the Messiah would bring a time when "the whole world will be occupied solely with the knowledge of God."[46] And, at last free to focus fully on the Divine, "the Children of Israel will be great sages; they will know hidden things and attain an understanding of their Creator to the extent of human capability."[47]

But for others, knowledge—even the deep and precious knowledge promised by Maimonides—was not enough. From the early medieval period some dared to envision a far more complete connection: a genuine union with the divine creation—and with the Divine Presence.

This anticipation sprang from the unique and fascinating beliefs of our mystics. Although many remained scrupulous in their ritual observance, these sages viewed God's nature—and God's creation—in a dramatically new way. They related to God as an incorporeal and limitless force uniting the universe, a divine pulse that flowed through the work of Creation.

But God's unifying power was not easily apprehended. Estrangement raged, isolation and conflict dividing creature from creature—and from communion with the divine spirit that sustained all. In order to return to the original and perfect unity of Creation, our mystics prescribed esoteric study, devotion, and practice. Through these acts, they held, we could overcome the separations that plagued this world and connect with the divine force that made everything one, achieving at last a literal unification with God and all that God had made.

And this union would blossom fully in the messianic time. Gershom Scholem writes:

> Only the redemption ... restores the utopian order ... in which the heart of life beats unconcealed and the isolation in which everything now finds itself is overcome.... The worlds will all be joined to one another, and nothing will separate Creator from creature.[48]

Redemption, therefore, meant redemption from the earthly torment of separation and a return to the first days of Creation, when all had been brought together in divine harmony and peace.

There is no single way, then, to relate to God in the Messianic Age. Yet each path culminates in the same glorious destination: an apprehension of and communion with the Divine and certainty that the One who created, sustained, and finally redeemed this world knows us and wants truly to be known by us as well.

What Is the Connection between Individual and Communal Redemption?

Until now, we have examined the messianic redemption as a universal, probably cataclysmic event. It would represent a complete break with history as we knew it, sparking either a return to the almost unimaginable primeval beauty of Creation or a hurtling forward into an age whose wonders we could barely conceive. Everything would appear renewed or altogether new. Everything would appear drastically changed. Everything—and everyone— would be affected.

Unless, of course, you believed otherwise.

We have seen that during the medieval period, as the scholarly and Rabbinic elite discouraged messianic speculation and attempted to tamp down fervent messianic longings, apocalyptic literature flourished among the general populace. In these years we also find a burgeoning community of Jewish mystics, who, dissatisfied with the rational, intellectual approach of the sages of their time, crafted an entirely new understanding of the nature of God and Creation and of the nature and purpose of salvation. Among their most important contributions to Jewish messianism stands the conviction that redemption can be an individual affair[49] and that the redemption of one soul can hasten the redemption of the universe.

Although messianism by definition would seem to look forward, we find our medieval kabbalists actually looking inward in search of redemption. They longed not for a glorious communal triumph *over* history but rather a peaceful individual escape *from* history. According to mystical teachings that flourished before 1492,[50] God and the divine creation are separated from one another by a series of rungs; the initiated, however, can learn to ascend these rungs and become at one with the Divine, turning away from the imperfections of this world and basking in reunion with God. "The kabbalist who was prepared to follow this path of inwardness," Scholem explains, "would be liberated and redeemed by the fact that he himself in the depths of his own soul would seek a way of return ... to the Source whence he was hewn."[51] A fifteenth-century text even interprets the traditional figures of Elijah and the Messiah as metaphors for an individual's capacity for salvation:

> Elijah is an allusion to the intellectual power, whereas [Messiah ben David] alludes to the prophetic power.... [The Messiah] will not indwell unless all the bodily powers and all the instincts be terminated—in other words be subjugated and acquiescent to the powers of intellect and prophecy.[52]

Moshe Idel clarifies that the Messiah "is not conceived of here to be an historical personality but rather simply a stage in the mystical development of a certain person."[53]

While intriguing, this focus on the individual might appear at odds with Judaism's emphasis on the community and its expectation of a universal redemption. And by the sixteenth century, our mystics had indeed come to link the salvation of a single person with the salvation of the world.

It was in the sixteenth century that Rabbi Isaac Luria, known also as the Ari, or "Lion," transformed Jewish mysticism. When we hear people speak today of Kabbalah, they are usually referring to Lurianic Kabbalah, his body of teachings that sought to explain the mysteries of Creation, exile, and redemption and brought mystical beliefs to the Jewish masses. Although scholars argue how acute an expectation of imminent deliverance the Ari held and the influence of that expectation among his followers, the contributions of Lurianic Kabbalah to the messianic vision are vast and undeniable. And perhaps most enduring among them is the assurance that each of us can make a difference—that each of us can help to bring redemption.

According to Lurianic Kabbalah, God planned to create the world through the use of sacred vessels that would hold the divine power. The mighty contents overwhelmed the vessels, however, causing them to shatter and scattering shards of divine light throughout Creation. Separated from one another and from their holy source, this light exists in painful exile—just as the universe, and each of us who dwells within it, lives isolated from the Divine and yearns for restoration and redemption.

But all is not lost. Through deeds of study, prayer, and piety, we are able to collect these divine sparks and, as it were, put them back together again. In doing so, we mend the brokenness in our lives; we feel the messianic light dawn within us, and our souls come to know wholeness and redemption. And there is yet more: when each individual soul has attained its individual redemption, the power of our collective souls is strong enough literally *l'taken olam*—to repair the world.[54]

While mystics differed on the exact nature of this salvation—Isaac Luria "envisioned an otherworldly redemption,"[55] for example, while later Hasidic mystics anticipated "a present redemption that may be consummated here"[56]—they agree on one extraordinary and groundbreaking image: individual achievement rather than supernatural intervention will be the hallmark of the Messianic Age. By the time the Messiah arrives, that is, he will no longer be needed; humanity will have done the work for him. The Messiah becomes "only a symbol for the completion of a process," Scholem states, "a testimony that the world has in fact been amended."[57]

And with a reduced role for the Messiah comes a dauntingly—yet inspiringly—expanded role for human beings. Rather than merely pray, or wait, or hope that God will take note of our faithfulness, we can act—and know that our actions matter in a deep and everlasting way. We can act—and encourage others to act with us. For every religious precept, every moment of learning, every act of loving-kindness holds cosmic significance; each becomes a prelude to deliverance, a gateway to welcoming the dominion of God and knowing the glory of the Divine.

CHAPTER SIX

The Messiah Is Us

As we begin to close our study of the Messiah, we may find mysticism reinvigorating our expectations and hopes. Mysticism appears to bridge the chasm between life as it is and as it should be; it offers us a clear vision of the universe redeemed—and an invitation to help make this vision a reality. Rather than embrace accounts of grisly battles or supernatural deeds, we can anticipate a world like this one, only much better. Rather than sit back and wait for salvation, we can work actively to achieve it. And rather than yearn for the Messiah, we can, as it were, become the Messiah.

But difficult issues remain. For redemption is so much bigger than we are; by definition, it transcends our history and our very selves. It demands not only that we feel we are making a contribution, but that that contribution is real, and enduring, and considerable. It calls us to work not independent of God, but in partnership with the Divine. And it insists that we never forget those generations who labored and suffered and died before us and that we refuse to be saved without them.

How, then, are we to envision ourselves as the Messiah? With clarity, and with humility. Mindful of our ancestors, their cherished visions and their deeply held beliefs, we dare not cast off the wisdom of the ages—even when it appears to conflict with our own. Mindful of our weakness, we dare not diminish the challenge of undoing all the evil humanity has wrought and enacting a deliverance greater than ourselves. And mindful of the vast and sacred nature of the messianic tasks, we dare not imagine we fulfill our role by dabbling in social justice or giving a few dollars to *tzedakah*[1] now and then.

But envisioning ourselves as the Messiah requires more than an honest assessment of the difficulty of achieving redemption. It compels us to acknowledge how painfully hard, how nearly impossible, the labors will be—and then try our best anyway. It reminds us that we are a people of tireless determination and inexhaustible hope and that if we work hard enough, and long enough, and passionately enough, perhaps we will come to earn the name "Messiah." And perhaps it will be we—who have witnessed the best and the worst humanity has fashioned and become—who shall prove instruments of the Divine and who shall know the privilege of bringing everlasting salvation to God's world, and ours.

Who Is the "Suffering Servant"?

Centuries before our mystics assigned a messianic role to the individual, the Jewish community was given an essential part to play in the drama of redemption. It was not a part many would embrace, but we have yet to cast it off completely.

In a famous biblical passage, the prophet Isaiah first introduced to the world God's "suffering servant":

> *He had no form or beauty, that we should regard him;*
> *   no charm, that we should find him pleasing.*
> *He was despised, shunned by humanity ... we held*
> *   him of no account.*
> *Yet it was our sickness that he was bearing, our suffering that he endured.*
> *We accounted him plagued, smitten and afflicted*
> *   by God—*
> *but he was wounded because of our sins, crushed*
> *   because of our iniquities.*
> *He bore the chastisement that made us whole,*
> *and by his bruises we were healed....*

He was maltreated, yet he was submissive; he did not
    open his mouth.
Like a sheep being led to slaughter; like an ewe,
    dumb before those that shear her,
he did not open his mouth....
Though he had done no injustice, and had spoken
    no falsehood....
If he made himself an offering for guilt ...
through him the Eternal's purpose might prosper.
    (Isaiah 53:2–5, 53:7, 53:9–10)[2]

A tragic figure, righteous but silently bearing the punishment for the sins of those who shun him, degraded and despised even as he ensures the wholeness of the world—we might easily fail to recognize ourselves in the miserable description. And yet the traditional understanding is unequivocal: the "suffering servant" of whom Isaiah speaks is the Jewish community, and our fate is indeed to suffer, and suffer horribly, that others might enjoy the blessings of deliverance.[3]

To be sure, this theme is not a central dogma in Jewish thought. Many have rejected the idea that suffering signifies atonement, redemption, or even punishment; particularly after the Holocaust, we may find it impossible to imagine any cause exalted enough to require so much human anguish. And we likely associate vicarious suffering—that one person or community can or should take on the transgressions of another—not with Judaism but with Christian belief.

Yet as discomfiting as we may find it, and as passionately as some may denounce it, the implication of the suffering servant remains part of our tradition. And for all of its horror, the image may bring a sort of solace, comforting us that our afflictions are not meaningless, not overlooked by God—that we do not suffer in vain. Rather than look upon ourselves as does the world—as possessed of "no form or beauty, that [they] should regard [us], no charm, that [they] should find [us] pleasing"—we can retain a sense of dignity, of nobility, of higher aspiration and destiny.

We can dare to ascribe to our people's pain the seeds of universal salvation.

Certainly some of our suffering ancestors clung to this view; we find it expressed in responses to communal tragedies across the ages, including the Crusades and even the Holocaust. And in one particularly haunting passage, our ancient sages—tormented horribly by their Roman oppressors—gave poignant new voice to Isaiah's vision:

> [At the time of king Messiah's creation], the Holy One will tell him in detail what will befall him: "These souls that have been put away with you—their sins will put you in a yoke of iron and make you like a calf whose eyes grow dim [with suffering]. They will strangle your breath with the yoke, and because of the sins of these souls, your tongue will cleave to the roof of your mouth. Are you willing to endure such trials?" ... And the Messiah will say: "Master of universes, I take this suffering upon myself with joy in my soul and gladness in my heart, so that not one person in Israel may perish."

And when the Messiah does reveal himself, the patriarchs Abraham, Isaac, and Jacob will greet him:

> "Our true Messiah, even though we are your forebears, you are greater than we.... For the sake of Israel you became a laughingstock and a derision among the nations of the earth, and you sat in darkness, in thick darkness, your eyes seeing no light, your skin cleaving to your bones, your body dry as a stick of wood, your teeth falling out from fasting, and your strength dried up like a potsherd." And he will reply: "O patriarchs, all that I have done, I have done only for your sake and for the sake of your children, that they may benefit from the goodness that the Holy One will bestow in abundance upon Israel."[4]

Regardless of how we feel about the nature and function of suffering, we are compelled to respect the convictions of those who came before us—those who personally withstood trials we cannot imagine and who painstakingly sought to reconcile their ordeals with their belief in a benevolent God and a purposeful universe. We may rightfully shudder, however, when we hear non-Jews utter similar sentiments, claiming to understand why our people have known such agony or daring to find in our suffering the keys to their own salvation. One powerful example: During a visit to Jerusalem in 1987, Cardinal John O'Connor proclaimed Jewish suffering at Auschwitz a "great gift" to the world; while his statement clearly reflected Isaiah's oracle, it was deservedly condemned by the Jewish community. Surely only ones who had survived the death camps, or who had lost their entire family to them, or who had experienced the full horror of the Nazi onslaught could possess the authority to speak this way. Such pronouncements were simply not Cardinal O'Connor's to make; he had not borne the suffering of the Jews at Auschwitz and therefore was not qualified to attempt to wrest meaning from it.

That the Jews have known more than our share of anguish is obvious and true. Whether this anguish signifies some greater purpose is far less clear. For those afflicted Jews who find individual comfort and inspiration in Isaiah's depiction of the suffering servant, well and good. But many of us do not accept that God intends to establish redemption upon the broken and burned bodies of the Jews, and we must not allow others to deny the terrible reality of Jewish suffering by taking refuge in such an image. The world at large may not exploit Isaiah's vision as a pat explanation for all we have endured—or excuse the persecution and slaughter of our people by calling it our "gift" to a yet unredeemed humanity.

What Is the Role of the Messiah in Hasidic Judaism?

In the middle of the eighteenth century, Hasidic Judaism was born. Founded by the legendary Rabbi Israel ben Eliezer—who came to be known as the Besht, an abbreviation for Ba'al Shem Tov, or "Good Master of the Holy Name"—Hasidism would challenge major movements in Judaism and emerge as one of the newest and most influential. Standing in sharp contrast to the Talmudists, whose fastidious devotion to text study precluded ardent prayer, and even the kabbalists, whose asceticism rendered them unable to experience fully the delights of this world, Hasidism combined traditional observance and a reinterpretation of Lurianic Kabbalah with a belief in God's immanent presence. And, perhaps most significant in a time when Eastern European Jewry had been physically and spiritually decimated by pogroms and persecutions, Hasidism proclaimed the inherent goodness of Creation and urged its followers to serve God with complete and utter joy.

The messianic expectations of Hasidism, however, remain unclear. Scholars differ on the nature of the deliverance envisioned by the Besht, and exactly how far off he supposed it to be. Some, most notably Gershom Scholem, argue that after the disastrous rise and fall of Shabbatei Zevi, Hasidism sought to "neutralize" messianic longing among its adherents by emphasizing individual communion with God over imminent universal salvation; and two other groups hold completely contradictory views, declaring either that Hasidism contains virtually no traditional messianic elements or that it actually reveals a major interest in messianism! Moshe Idel persuasively reminds that what we call Hasidism comprises a tremendous variety of teachings, leaders, and messianic models, making it impossible to identify a single, unified Hasidic perspective on the subject of redemption.[5]

Still, we can draw some basic generalizations. The redemption of Hasidism is rarely an apocalyptic redemption; there are few calamitous messianic birth pangs, calls to arms, bloodstained victories at the gates of Jerusalem. Rather, Hasidic messianism blossomed quite naturally from Hasidic convictions about God, about the nature of the world and the duties of humanity. Hasids sought a unique form of communion with God known as *devekut*—a literal cleaving to or feeling at one with the Divine—and found this act akin to redemption. Redefining familiar messianic terms such as *galut* (exile) and *ge'ulah* (redemption), Egypt (the nation of our enslavement) and Israel (the land of our freedom), in more spiritual terms,[6] Hasidism enabled its followers to see salvation as a possibility for every individual. By leaving our own Egypt (the state that blinds us to God's presence and God's goodness) and overcoming our own *galut* (our own exile from the Divine), they taught, we can come to know *ge'ulah* (redemption from our limits and shortcomings) and thrive in Israel—a place of joyfully engaging in God's commandments and apprehending the nearness of the Eternal.

This deliverance would be accomplished not by mourning the imperfections of the universe, nor by denying oneself its pleasures, nor by employing theurgic or magical rituals, nor by woodenly participating in study and worship, but by embracing this world and finding ecstasy and fulfillment and divinity in doing God's will within it. Heartfelt prayer and deeds became the necessary tools for redemption; not only ritual but ethical and social acts were transformed into messianic principles. Salvation would require doing—and doing with joy.

And while the Besht echoed the kabbalists in his assertion that a universal redemption would have to wait until every human being had achieved redemption—or at least, according to one legend, until his own teachings had spread all over the world[7]—the opportunity for individual deliverance was already plenty to celebrate. The modern theologian Leo Baeck explains:

> By being open to the fact that redemption always and everywhere has its place and its day, and that something that strives to be redeemed waits for every [person], messianism, the great expectation, the great hope, won a constant actuality. The touch of greatness entered narrow existence.[8]

And Martin Buber exults:

> If you direct the undiminished power of your fervor to God's world-destiny, if you do what you must do at this moment— no matter what it may be!—with your whole strength and with *kavannah*, with holy intent—you will bring about the union between God and *Shechinah* [the Divine Presence], eternity and time.[9]

As Hasidism grew, and spread, and developed, different sects arose. Each had its own unique set of teachings and its own *tzaddikim*, "righteous ones"[10] who functioned as both charismatic spiritual leaders and—according to Hasidic belief—vessels from which God's light would flow. Legends and miracle stories sprang up around these *tzaddikim*; some were even credited with messianic qualities and viewed as potential redeemers. Shot by a Cossack as he led Shabbat services in the synagogue, the dying Rabbi Shelomo—at whose prayer "the springs of [his disciples'] spirits gushed forth, [and] the spirit possessed them so utterly that until long after the Sabbath they did not know the difference between day and night"—was identified with the Messiah ben Joseph;[11] the Hasidic rabbi of Kalev's pleas for redemption proved forceful enough to call the patriarchs and matriarchs down from heaven;[12] and two *tzaddikim* held power over the souls of the dead.[13] While none of these *tzaddikims* was truly regarded as the Messiah—and while none sought the title—such tales illuminate their perceived proximity to the Divine and the wondrous possibility that salvation lay well within the reach of humanity.

When we consider today the place of messianism in Hasidic Judaism, however, we likely find our minds turning to the best known and most influential group of modern Hasids—that of Chabad-Lubavitch. And while the history and narratives of earlier Hasids considering and seeking redemption fascinate in their own right, they take on a new significance in light of the work of Chabad—and the mesmerizing figure of Rabbi Menachem Mendel Schneerson.

Who Is Rabbi Schneerson?

According to thousands of followers, Rabbi Menachem Mendel Schneerson is the Messiah.

According to virtually everyone else, he has been dead since 1994; yet he remains the center of the most fascinating—and vexing—messianic movement of modern times.

All can agree at least on this: In 1951, Rabbi Menachem Mendel Schneerson was installed as the seventh leader—the Rebbe—of

Chabad-Lubavitch, a Hasidic sect that originated in Belorussia and whose elite fled to America during the Holocaust.[14] Under his guidance Chabad transformed from a little-known Jewish sect into a religious force recognized around the world. Chabad itself, however, became a source of tremendous controversy. Supporters lauded its sense of tradition, spirituality, and purpose, welcoming outreach, good works for non-Jews, and free services; while detractors protested its denial of equality for all, public displays of religious symbols, interference in Israeli politics, and aggressive fundraising and recruitment.

But even the most passionate critics found it difficult to repudiate the Rebbe completely. For one thing, he simply accomplished so much. Turning on its head the image of an insular Jewish community and a remote rabbinate, Rabbi Schneerson for years personally greeted thousands of people every Sunday; he oversaw the opening of treatment centers for Jewish and non-Jewish drug addicts and an enormous expansion of prison ministry. He also enjoyed wide regard in the secular world; Hollywood notables like Jon Voight and Jerry Weintraub appeared at his Chabad fundraisers, and he even received a posthumous Congressional Gold Medal. Perhaps his most famous innovations, however, were "*mitzvah* campaigns" to bring Jewish customs to Jews wherever they might be found (if, for example, you have ever been accosted at Tel Aviv's Ben-Gurion Airport by a young Chabadnik inviting you to lay tefillin, you have the Rebbe to thank—or blame, depending on your perspective!) and the *shlichim* (emissaries)[15] program, which sent thousands of young Lubavitchers to minister to Jews all over the world—from Los Angeles and Miami to Singapore and Japan, from Arkansas and Massachusetts to Paraguay and the Congo.

What was the role of messianism in Rabbi Schneerson's work? Of course he subscribed to the Hasidic tenet that humanity's deeds influence the Messiah's arrival, but under his leadership Chabad went much further than that. He loudly and repeatedly called for the Messiah's advent; signs bellowing "We Want *Moshiach* Now!"[16]

and newspaper ads predicting imminent redemption became ubiquitous. And he made his view most explicit in pronouncements
like these: "This is the last generation of exile and the first generation of redemption!" "Humble ones, the time of your redemption
has arrived!" and, in a famous 1991 speech, "I have done everything I can. Now I am handing [it] over to you: Do everything you
can to bring *Moshiach*!"

The Rebbe's messianic yearning proved infectious. The fervor, however, soon came to focus on Rabbi Schneerson himself.

Although some Lubavitchers had long entertained the idea
that Rabbi Schneerson might be the Messiah, such speculation
intensified in 1992, when he suffered a devastating stroke that
paralyzed his right side and rendered him completely speechless.
No longer able to talk, the incapacitated Rebbe merely looked
on, neither encouraging nor discouraging, as followers gathered
beneath his window and chanted, "*Melech HaMoshiach*" (the King
Messiah), and proclaimed him throughout the world as God's
anointed. In his last days, his inner circle even debated how much
medical intervention to pursue; should he receive state-of-the-art
medical treatment or be left alone in case his afflictions were a
necessary part of his messianic character? (The Rebbe was taken
to the hospital.)

Even after the Rebbe passed away, his identification as
redeemer did not end. In a startling development, thousands
of Chabadniks—appropriately dubbed messianists—continued
to venerate him, anticipating his resurrection and revelation as
King Messiah. Nor was the phenomenon short-lived. Two years
after Rabbi Schneerson's death, these messianists erected a bill-
board over the George Washington Bridge heralding his return;
in 1998 they held a "*Moshiach* congress" that featured posters
and chocolate bars bearing the Rebbe's image; and in the 2000s
they plastered Israel—from the fortress of Masada to the streets
of Jerusalem—with stickers bearing the Rebbe's face and the
words *Yechi HaMelech HaMoshiach*, "The King Messiah Will Live."
Undeterred by warnings that their reverence for a deceased leader

would put them outside the accepted boundaries of Judaism,[17] at least through 2012 they continued to press their case that Rabbi Schneerson was the Messiah.[18]

While Chabad's leadership dismissed the messianists as a fringe group, the claim—and its adherents—was not easy to shake. Among the messianists were prominent figures such as Rabbi Shmuel Butman, head of both the Lubavitch Youth Organization and the International Campaign to Bring *Moshiach,* and like any good Chabadniks, he and his followers proved amazingly adept at getting their message out through the secular media and word of mouth. And mainstream Chabad itself remained suffused with messianism, publishing a children's magazine called the *Moshiach Times,* speaking about the Rebbe in the present tense,[19] and declining to appoint a living successor to Rabbi Schneerson. The issue continues to arise. In 2008, for example, popular singer Matisyahu explained that Lubavitch's messianic teachings had driven him from the movement; and a rabbinical court in Jerusalem was reported to refuse conversion for a would-be proselyte who declared a belief that Rabbi Schneerson was the Messiah.

Chabad's official position, however, is to deny that such episodes represent its true character. Even Rabbi Yehuda Krinsky, the Lubavitch leader once counted among the Rebbe's closest associates, asserted four years after Rabbi Schneerson's death, "No one can know with certainty, and clearly should not campaign about, who *Moshiach* may or may not be."[20]

What Did Classical Reform Judaism Teach about the Messiah?

In 1848 something amazing happened: the Jews of Germany were emancipated.

We who had citizenship conferred upon us at birth or who earned citizenship by following a clear and straightforward path may find it difficult to imagine the enormity of this event. Although they had lived on the continent of Europe for two millennia, pre-Emancipation Jews had never been citizens; they enjoyed no inherent rights or privileges, and they had virtually no recourse when the nation in which they were living turned against them. Finally to be emancipated—to receive full citizenship, to be granted political rights—was, for many, an experience akin to redemption.

At last fabled German society lay open to her Jews: the arts and culture, the literature and thought, the science and intellect, the sophistication and majesty. But traditional Jewish life remained inward looking, insular, suspicious and dismissive of the outside world. How might the two be reconciled? How might one become an authentic German but still live as an authentic Jew?

"Reform Judaism" proved a compelling answer. Born in Germany during the days of Emancipation, Reform Judaism sought to preserve—and enhance—the most precious elements of Judaism in the face of modernity's opportunities and challenges, and it applied the era's values of rationality, optimism, and universality to religious life.[21] Although a discussion of Reform Judaism's impact could fill—and has in fact filled!—countless books, we will focus here on only one aspect: its redefinition of the Messiah and the Messianic Age.

For traditional Jewish views on the Messiah could not, early Reformers believed, possibly stand in this time of Emancipation. A scientific, intellectual study of Judaism was taking hold; reason and rationally articulated convictions were prized. And clearly messianism as our forebears knew it—marked by apocalyptic battles, supernatural saviors, and resurrected dead, rooted in complicated scriptural allusions and mythical folklore—did not fit. Nor was messianism conducive to full and enthusiastic participation in secular society; if emancipated Jews continued to envision salvation as a radical break from everything this world had to offer, after all, how could they appreciate the advantages newly bestowed upon them? With its emphasis on Jewish vindication and triumph, messianism also sharply contradicted the Emancipation's tenet of universalism. And, finally, messianism endangered the Jews' new status as loyal citizens. How faithful to Germany could the Jews really be, an opponent of Emancipation might argue, when they were constantly proclaiming their yearning for Zion?

But perhaps the most powerful reason to jettison traditional messianic belief, the Reformers argued, was that *it was simply not needed anymore*. Human beings—guided not by a heaven-sent figure but by their own intellect, conscience, and imagination—had already begun to accomplish the work of redemption.[22] Emancipation was only the beginning, they believed; its principles and its energy would spread across nations and oceans, lighting up the darkness of ignorance and oppression, healing the wounds of uncaring and injustice, eventually bringing liberation to every corner of the earth. There was no need for divine intervention or even assistance; bound by common humanity and united in a single purpose, people were at last working together to redeem their own selves, their own society—their own world.[23]

The German Reformers' convictions echoed strongly with many nineteenth-century American Jews, who recognized in their own freedom and opportunity the promise of redemption. No longer seeking a personal messiah, a restoration to Zion, the rebuilding of the Temple in Jerusalem, or a physical resurrection, they too began to understand salvation as a human enterprise and to define it simply as extending to the world the blessings they themselves already enjoyed in the United States. Their leaders made this abundantly clear in the Pittsburgh Platform of 1885, the original statement of principles of American Reform Judaism:

> We recognize, in the modern era of universal culture of heart and intellect, the approaching of the realization of Israel's great messianic hope for the establishment of the kingdom of truth, justice, and peace among all.... We expect neither a return to Palestine, nor a sacrificial worship under the sons of Aaron.... We reject as ideas not rooted in Judaism, the beliefs both in bodily resurrection and in ... abodes for everlasting punishment and reward.[24]

Reform prayer books throughout Europe and the United States reflected these declarations. Worshippers reciting the *Amidah* no longer awaited a *go'el*, "redeemer," but *ge'ulah*, "redemption"; they acclaimed God not as *mechayei hametim*, "Resurrector of the dead," but as *mechayei hakol*, "Giver of life to all"; and they petitioned God not for the ingathering of the exiles, the rebuilding of Jerusalem, and the restoration of the Davidic monarchy, but for universal liberty, justice, and a sense of God's nearness. Although these innovations date to the nineteenth century, virtually all are still part of liberal Jewish liturgy today; in fact, among the most controversial elements in the creation of the prayer book *Mishkan T'filah*, issued by American Reform movement in 2007, was the question of whether to reintroduce the phrase *mechayei hametim*, "Resurrector of the dead."

Many critiques of early Reform Judaism fault its progenitors for abandoning the ritual aspects of Jewish tradition, the spirituality and mysticism, the wonder and mystery. Yet classical Reform brought marvelous gifts: a path to stand as a rational, engaged member of society and a believing Jew; a way to adapt Jewish wisdom to the age's new challenges; and, perhaps most significant, a call for all humanity to bring the messianic promise to full and magnificent realization—to embrace emancipation, liberation, and universalism and to repair together all the brokenness in our world.

Of course, that great hope would not come to pass. For only half a century later would the naïve optimism of classical Reform's leaders become tragically clear.

What Does Modern Liberal Judaism Teach about the Messiah?

Classical Reform Judaism's messianism could not stand in the shadow of the Holocaust; Auschwitz made a devastating mockery of the idea that civilization was progressing quickly and inevitably toward universal liberation. Who could any longer echo the classical Reformers' buoyant optimism, their easy faith in people's goodness, their sanguine confidence that salvation lay within our reach?

But what was left? Having rejected the traditional tenets of divine intervention, a personal redeemer, and a messianic future rooted in the restoration of Zion, liberal Jews had cast their lot with humanity ... and humanity had thrown their brothers and sisters into crematoria. The redemption envisaged by their ancestors was not the redemption they sought, but the redemption they sought, they now understood, could never be achieved.

Modern Jewish messianism has still not absorbed this blow. Sixty-five years after the liberation of Auschwitz, liberal Judaism has yet to articulate a clear and compelling messianic vision.[25]

A look at its liturgy and platforms, however, may not reveal the problem. Beautiful language and stirring sentiments pervade them all; we "hope to behold the perfection of our world, guided by a sacred Covenant drawn from human and divine meeting"[26] and ask to "soon behold the glory of Your might ... perfecting the world under the rule of God."[27] Modern Judaism, we proclaim, "abhors all violence and relies upon moral education, love and sympathy to secure human progress."[28] And "we continue to have faith that, in spite of the unspeakable evils committed against our people and the sufferings endured by others, the partnership of God and humanity will ultimately prevail."[29]

The words soothe, console, and inspire, but what do they really mean? Are we imploring God to reveal "the glory of Your might," as did the author of *Sefer Zerubbabel*, or do we "[abhor] all violence"—even that which might be necessary to achieve the cause of redemption? How will a "sacred Covenant drawn from human and divine meeting" reach those who deny the reality of God? And as humanity continues to perpetrate slaughter and war, cruelty and abuse, can we truly be so certain that "the partnership of God and humanity will ultimately prevail"?

Not only the official declarations of liberal Judaism but the actions of liberal Jews reflect this uncertainty. For many, the messianic enterprise has been redefined as participation in community service and the promise that each of us can become a savior. These Jews speak of "repairing the world" as they raise money for *tzedakah*, build homes for Habitat for Humanity, or lobby on behalf of Darfur's refugees; rather than emphasizing its complex and esoteric aspects, they employ the term *tikkun olam* as a synonym for social justice. And their labors, according to some, do indeed portend messianic rewards: "The actual work of redeeming the world is turned to us in history, and is done by all of us, day by day," writes modern theologian Arthur Green. "Rather than messiah redeeming us, we redeem messiah."[30] And in the provocatively titled *There Is No Messiah and You're It*, Robert N. Levine charges, "God anointed every one of us. You don't have to wring your hands.... What are all you messiahs waiting for?"[31]

To be sure, this concept of messianism appeals and rouses. With a wink to the narcissism of our time, it extols each of us as special, honored, praiseworthy; and, more significant, in the spirit of mysticism it impels us to do all we can to achieve justice and kindness. Yet it still fails to provide a complete vision of salvation or to explain how relatively isolated acts of goodness can overcome the tyranny and hatred plaguing so much of our world. As theologian Abraham Joshua Heschel asks, "If Judaism had relied exclusively on the human resources for the good, on [humanity]'s ability to fulfill what God demands, on [humanity]'s power to achieve redemption, why did it insist upon the promise of *messianic* redemption?"[32] The work described as *tikkun olam* is sacred and significant and should not be denigrated, but neither should it be equated with the redemption of the universe and the reign of the Messiah.

Other liberal Jews have explored more spiritual facets of messianism. Seeking the individual redemption anticipated by our mystics or a traditional framework in which to become agents of redemption, they yearn for more than the vague messianism liberal Judaism articulates. Although they continue to identify themselves as liberal Jews, many flock to classes and organizations outside the mainstream Jewish community—from Chabad lectures and Kabbalah seminars to meditation circles and Buddhist retreats. After all, what questing Jew wouldn't be enticed by the Kabbalah Centre's pledge: "Kabbalah shows in detail how to ... remove every form of chaos, pain and suffering.... Its purpose is to bring clarity, understanding, and freedom ... and ultimately to erase even death itself."[33] Jewish author Sylvia Boorstein found a similar allure in Buddhism: "From the very first time I heard the Buddha's elegant and succinct teaching about the possibility of the end of suffering," she writes, "I was captivated, I was thrilled, and I was reassured."[34]

In our age of cynicism and turmoil, it is difficult to criticize those who have embraced the promise of deliverance. And many Jews who explore these other paths do return to liberal Judaism infused with new spirituality and passion for good works. Yet it is distressing that so many feel driven to look elsewhere for a compelling messianic message. It is painful to watch them leaving liberal Judaism in search of "clarity, understanding, and freedom," and to see them "captivated ... thrilled, and ... reassured" by a faith not theirs. And it is tragic that they have never been taught their own heritage—that for nearly three millennia their people have served as oracles of the messianic vision and guardians of the messianic hope.

While neither traditional nor classical Reform teachings may speak to liberal Jews today, still liberal Judaism dare not abandon the messianism that gives Judaism—and perhaps our lives and our world—import and meaning, beauty and significance. Somehow we must look at our past, at our present, and within ourselves and find a way to echo the words of Maimonides, and the chant of our people at the gates of Auschwitz: "Even with all this, I will await [the Messiah] every day."

Can We Experience the Messiah?

As we have seen, our ancestors maintained a messianic hope spanning nearly three millennia, exalted expectations ranging from a rebuilt Temple to a reborn universe, and thrice-daily prayers imploring God to hasten the time of deliverance. So we might be shocked at their answer to this question: Yes. In fact, we can experience the Messiah every week.

How? Through the observance of Shabbat.

According to Jewish tradition, God intends the weekly Sabbath not merely as rest, not merely as religious obligation, but as a foretaste of redemption. In the spirit of Shabbat, Judaism teaches, are the joy and the peace of the Messianic Age.

The rituals and ceremonies of Shabbat expressly foreshadow the days of deliverance. The elaborate Shabbat dinner parallels the Feast of the Righteous, the shunning of work corresponds to the era's endless serenity and abundance, and the prayers and songs herald a time when all shall know the Divine Presence. But even we who may not keep a traditional Sabbath can still come to know a taste of salvation. As the messianic Shabbat hymn *Lecha Dodi* urges: "Come with me to meet Shabbat, forever a fountain of blessing.... Awake, awake, your light has come! The Eternal's glory dawns upon you.... An end to shame and degradation; forget your sorrow; quiet your groans.... As a bridegroom rejoices in his beloved, your God takes joy in you."[35]

How marvelous to sing of "an end to shame and degradation," to feel "the Eternal's glory dawn upon" us, to draw near to the Divine as one "rejoices in his [or her] beloved." How marvelous to recall the perfection and the unity of Creation and the rest that came after. How marvelous to look forward to the restoration of that perfection and that unity and to the endless delight that will follow.

❋

I did not learn about this interpretation of Shabbat until I was in rabbinical school. I wish I had learned it earlier.

I wish I had learned a lot about the Messiah earlier. I hope that we can learn it now.

I hope that we can begin to talk about the Messiah, and redemption, and the promise that our history and our universe and our lives resonate with meaning and purpose. I hope that we can approach the topic of messianism not with uncertainty or embarrassment but with openness, curiosity, and fascination. I hope that we can hold classes and hear sermons and offer prayers that speak of the Messiah and our ancestors' various and wondrous visions of salvation. I hope that we can grapple with the challenges of believing without concluding that it's just too difficult, or too irrational, or too foreign to our experience thus far. I hope that we can infuse community service and social action projects with a sense that we are perhaps acting as agents of deliverance.

I hope that while we may not be certain what form redemption will take, or when it will arrive, or why it has taken so long, we can find the conviction and the courage to join the generations upon generations who have for nearly three thousand years kept faith with the Messiah.

And I hope that we can open ourselves to acknowledge what I believe we are already doing—experiencing the Messiah.

For when we witness the suffering in our world and find every reason to despair, but we do not despair, I believe it is because somewhere deep within us burns the hope for redemption. When we designate for the needy funds we might wish to spend on ourselves, or volunteer hours we might prefer to while away, or speak out when we might take refuge in uneasy silence, I believe it is because we sense the messianic promise. And when we aspire to something higher and feel the glimmering of union between our souls and the Divine, the encounter of the people we are with the people we wish to be, the meeting of the universe we inhabit with the universe God so long ago declared "very good"—I believe we are anticipating the time of salvation.

The ancient Greeks and Romans who once conquered our ancestors looked to the past, saw their shining histories as the Golden Age of the universe. But our people has always looked forward. Our people has always waited for something more. Our people has always waited for the Messiah.

※

A Talmudic sage named Raba once taught that after we die, we appear before God to account for how we spent our time in this world.[36] God wants to hear about our actions—what we did and what we discussed, if we behaved with honor and conducted ourselves with integrity. Then God poses one more question, and it is perhaps the hardest one: Did you, God asks, did you hope for redemption?

Of course we don't know if this conversation will ever really take place. (And even if it does, we might assume God already knows the answer!) But isn't it telling that of all the questions God might ask about our inner life—whether we ever entertained a belief in another deity, or lusted in our hearts, or spaced out during religious services—our ancestors imagined only one: Did you hope for redemption?

Why? Maybe because if we can keep our hope for redemption intact after a lifetime of witnessing the imperfections of this world, we deserve all the heavenly reward God can give. Maybe because hoping for redemption enables us to live the way we deserve to live: with faith, and trust, and conviction that things will get better than this. Or maybe because even if we don't live to see it, we deserve to experience the amazing and wonderful and exhilarating certainty that the Messiah will come.

Modern philosopher Emil Fackenheim speaks about the messianic hope like this: "I think you have to hold onto it even if you can't say what is going to be.... [For] where there is hope there is life. And when there is life there is hope."[37]

Emil Fackenheim was not only a philosopher. He was also attacked by the Nazis on *Kristallnacht*[38] and imprisoned in the Sachsenhausen concentration camp.

Even with all this, we await the Messiah every day.

AUTHOR'S NOTE

"The time is at hand when I shall bring about something entirely new."[1]

Even with all the citations, references, and footnotes, this is actually a very personal book! I am grateful to everyone who helped me bring it into being and bring it to you—and I am grateful to you, for reading, for considering, and maybe even for believing.

I'd like to express deep appreciation to Stuart Matlins, Emily Wichland, and the entire team at Jewish Lights Publishing for giving this book wonderful life in the world beyond my laptop, and to Rabbis Judith Abrams and Neil Gillman for their beautiful contributions. I also offer sincerest thanks to Rabbis and Professors Edward Goldman, Barry Kogan, Michael Meyer, and Richard Sarason, and Rabbis Edwin Goldberg, Yitz Greenberg, Hara Person, and Moishe Traxler, for instruction and inspiration, as well as the staff of the Hebrew Union College–Jewish Institute of Religion's libraries in Cincinnati, Los Angeles, and New York, and the incomparable faculty and students of the Shalom Hartman Institute in Jerusalem. I benefitted intellectually and spiritually from visits to the Shrine of the Book, Arbel National Park, the Teomim Cave, Hebrew Union College–Jerusalem, and other sites throughout the Holy Land of Israel in the summer of 2012. Thank you, finally, to Judy and Albert Glickman, Helen and Larry Rose, Sharon Kunkel, Alicia Zoller, and (most especially and always) Brenner Glickman, for believing in this project and in me.

In the midst of its ferocious visions and chilling prophecies, the seventh-century apocalypse *Sefer Zerubbabel* holds one of the simplest and most beautiful blessings I have ever received. May its words be fulfilled for the good, for all of us and ours:

"May God grant that we merit to behold ... our righteous Messiah, speedily in our days. Amen amen amen, *selah selah selah.*"[2]

NOTES

Introduction

1. Camus places this statement, ironically enough, in the mouth of ancient Jewry's great enemy Caligula. Albert Camus, *Caligula and Three Other Plays*, trans. Stuart Gilbert (New York: Vintage Books, 1958), p. 8.

2. BCE stands for "before the Common Era," an equivalent of BC, or "before Christ." Jews frequently substitute BCE for BC, and CE (Common Era) for AD (*anno Domini*, "the year of our Lord") in order to avoid implicitly referring to Jesus as a divine figure.

3. *Sifra, Behukotai* 2, in Joseph Klausner, *The Messianic Idea in Israel*, trans. W. F. Stinespring (New York: Macmillan, 1955), p. 511.

4. Talmud, *Ketubot* 111b, in Klausner, *Messianic Idea*, p. 508.

5. In Judaism, Diaspora generally refers to lands other than Israel.

CHAPTER ONE

The Messiah Is Coming!

1. Midrash, which means "teaching" or "explication," refers to Rabbinic interpretations of sacred texts and traditions. The midrashim (plural of midrash) related to the Messiah are often imaginative and fanciful and are not always to be understood literally.

2. *Pesikta Rabbati*, Friedmann edition, p. 152b, in Raphael Patai, *The Messiah Texts* (Detroit: Wayne State University Press, 1979), p. 19. A humorous anachronism may be noted in at least two sources describing a prehistorical Messiah: Though obviously preceding King David by millennia, the Messiah is nonetheless identified as the Messiah ben David. See Joseph Jacobs and Moses Buttenwieser, "Messiah," in *Jewish Encyclopedia*, www.jewishencyclopedia.com/articles/10729-messiah.

3. Moshe Idel, *Messianic Mystics* (New Haven, CT: Yale University Press, 1998), pp. 189–190. He interprets the proper name Adam as the acronym *ADM*, or *aleph, dalet, mem*, initials for the three names Adam,

David, and Messiah. The relationship between King David and the Messiah is discussed fully in chap. 2.

4. The Elijah cited here is the same prophet who plays a central role in the first book of Kings. According to the Bible (2 Kings 2:1–12), Elijah did not die but was taken up to heaven alive in a fiery chariot. Later stories describe his returning to earth in order to help, comfort, and judge the Jewish people. He also holds an essential place in messianic tradition, which is discussed later in this chapter and in chaps. 3 and 5.

5. *B'reshit Rabbati*, pp. 130–131, adapted from Patai, *Messiah Texts*, p. 124.

6. In Edwin Cole Goldberg, "Book of Zerubbal" (rabbinic thesis, Hebrew Union College–Jewish Institute of Religion, 1989), p. 11.

7. Ibid, pp. 58, 160. The image of the Messiah living among Israel's enemies intentionally recalls Moses's early life in the house of Pharaoh. Just as Moses fled Egypt before helping to redeem his people from slavery, so will the Messiah break free from his land before revealing himself as Israel's savior.

8. In *Pesikta Rabbati*, Friedmann edition, pp. 146b–147a, in Patai, *Messiah Texts*, pp. 183–184.

9. In *Maasei diRabbi Joshua ben Levi*, BhM 2:49–50, in Patai, *Messiah Texts*, p. 135.

10. *Zohar* 2:8a–9a, in Patai, *Messiah Texts*, pp. 85–89. The *Zohar*, translated as "[The Book of] Splendor," is the crowning work of medieval mysticism. Presented as a commentary on the Torah, the *Zohar* comprises the greatest wealth of cosmological and theosophical teachings in Jewish tradition. The collection was presented and possibly authored by Moses de Leon in the late thirteenth century, although the work is traditionally ascribed to famed second-century rabbi Shimon bar Yochai.

11. *Ruth Rabbah* 5:6. A similar teaching appears in *Leviticus Rabbah* 35:8.

12. "Biblical" and "Bible" refer throughout this book specifically to the Hebrew Bible, often known to non-Jews as the Old Testament. Jews also call it the *Tanakh*, an abbreviation for its three sections: *Torah*, *Nevi'im* (Prophets), and *Ketuvim* (Holy Writings). While Christians usually interpret the Hebrew Bible through the lens of the Gospels and Paul's epistles, Jews traditionally do so through Rabbinic commentaries contained in the Talmud and midrash.

13. Talmud, *Pesachim* 13a, in David S. Ariel, *What Do Jews Believe? The Spiritual Foundations of Judaism* (New York: Schocken Books, 1995), p. 224.

14. *Mechilta deRabbi Ishmael, pischa* 14, in Ariel, *What Do Jews Believe?*, p. 224 and *Sefer Zerubbabel*, as cited on placard at Arbel National Park,

Israel. Passover celebrates the Israelites' deliverance from slavery in Egypt and serves as a paradigm for the Jewish experience of redemption.

15. In Ephraim E. Urbach, *The Sages: Their Concepts and Beliefs*, trans. Israel Abrahams (Jerusalem: Magnes Press, 1987), pp. 671–672. On the first day of Tishrei Jews observe Rosh Hashanah—literally, "the Head of the Year," and traditionally the date on which God created humanity.

16. The Talmud, whose title comes from the Hebrew root meaning "learn" or "study," stands as one of the central and most essential treasures of Jewish teaching. It comprises two parts: the Mishnah, a series of discussions and rulings on Jewish law, and the Gemara, an extended commentary on the Mishnah. Although the Talmud is often defined as a legal code, the work comprises not only interpretations of the Torah's statutes but also a wealth of narrative, liturgy, theology, fable, and legend. There are two versions of the Talmud: the Jerusalem Talmud, likely codified around the fifth century, and the more comprehensive Babylonian Talmud, likely codified a century later.

17. Abba Hillel Silver, *A History of Messianic Speculation in Israel* (Gloucester, MA: Peter Smith, 1978), p. 68.

18. Ibid., pp. 75–76.

19. Ibid., p. 60.

20. An interesting exception is Rashi, Rabbi Shlomo Yitzhaki, the vaunted eleventh-century sage whose teachings and commentaries are arguably the most authoritative in Jewish tradition; Joseph Sarachek, *The Doctrine of the Messiah in Medieval Jewish Literature* (New York: Jewish Theological Society of America, 1932), p. 59.

21. Talmud, *Sanhedrin* 97a, in Gershom Scholem, *The Messianic Idea in Judaism* (London: George Allen & Unwin, 1971), p. 11.

22. *Avot deRabbi Natan* 31b.

23. *Derech Eretz Rabbah*, chap. 11, in Joseph Klausner, *The Messianic Idea in Israel*, trans. W. F. Stinespring (New York: Macmillan, 1955), p. 425.

24. *Sefer Hasidim*, Margoliot edition, p. 195, no. 206; Wistinetzki and Friedmann edition, no. 212, in Idel, *Messianic Mystics*, p. 49.

25. Maimonides, *Yad HaHazakah, Shofetim, Hilchot Melachim* 11–12, in Patai, *Messiah Texts*, p. 326.

26. Our generation has proved no exception; in the March/April 2012 issue of *Moment*, the ultra-Orthodox rabbi Abraham J. Twerski and the internationally heralded *rebbetzin* Esther Jungreis referred to the Holocaust, the rebirth of Israel, moral degeneration, the rise of Islam,

and Iran's work to develop nuclear weapons as signs heralding what Twerski called "the imminent coming of the Messiah" (pp. 25, 32).

27. In Silver, *History of Messianic Speculation*, p. 75.

28. There have been notable exceptions to this rule, however. Some mystics have employed theurgic acts—supposed magic that can force God's hand—in attempts to bring the Messiah. Such practices include prayers, incantations, recitations of the divine name, and self-mortification, including fasting. If they performed these acts in exactly the right manner, these messianists believed, God would be compelled to send the Messiah. A fascinating survey of their deeds can be found in Patai, *Messiah Texts*, chap. 7. Even in modern times, fringe groups plot to rebuild the Temple in Jerusalem and reinstate biblical animal sacrifice in order to coerce the Messiah's arrival.

29. *Sanhedrin* 98a, adapted from Patai, *Messiah Texts*, p. 110. Elijah's rejoinder to Rabbi Joshua quotes Psalm 95:7.

30. Kabbalah, which literally means "receiving," refers to a tremendous body of Jewish mystical literature, tradition, and teaching. A kabbalist is a student of or believer in this material.

31. In Silver, *History of Messianic Speculation*, p. 235. Italics are mine.

32. *Midrash HaNeelam* in *Zohar Hadash*, f. 23d, in Gershom Scholem, *Major Trends in Jewish Mysticism* (New York: Schocken Books, 1941), p. 250.

33. Talmud, *Shabbat* 118b, in Klausner, *Messianic Idea in Israel*, p. 427.

34. *Exodus Rabbah* 25:16, in Scholem, *Messianic Idea in Judaism*, p. 11.

35. Talmud, *Sanhedrin* 98a.

36. *Song of Songs Rabbah* 6:10, in Scholem, *Messianic Idea in Judaism*, pp. 10–11.

37. Talmud, *Sanhedrin* 96b–97a, and *Targum* to 1 Chronicles 3:24, in Patai, *Messiah Texts*, pp. 82–83.

38. *IV Ezra* 13:1ff, in Patai, *Messiah Texts*, p. 82.

39. *Pirkei Mashiach*, BhM 3:70, in Patai, *Messiah Texts*, p. 83. The biblical text that follows "as it is written ..." is the prophecy described earlier in the paragraph; the text is Daniel 7:13.

40. The Gospel of Matthew's influential statement that "all the peoples of the world will ... see the Son of Man coming on the clouds of heaven with great power and glory"—an echo of Daniel 7:13—may also have contributed to the deemphasizing of this tradition. See Matthew 24:30ff.

41. *The "Ethiopic" Book of Enoch* 90:17ff, in Klausner, *Messianic Idea in Israel*, p. 288. This tradition is also cited in Jacobs and Buttenwieser,

"Messiah," where the source is called *The Visions of the Seventy Shepherds of the Book of Enoch* and identified as "the first [apocalyptic] book to be mentioned in which the Messiah figures as an earthly king." Apocalyptic literature is discussed fully in chap. 3.

42. The famous depiction of the Messiah riding a donkey through the Golden Gate of Jerusalem is rooted in this text.

43. Talmud, *Sanhedrin* 98b, in Patai, *Messiah Texts*, p. 20.

44. The founder of Hasidic Judaism. He and the movement he birthed are discussed fully in chap. 6.

45. From Kadaner, *Sefer Sippurim Noraim*, pp. 9a–9b, 10b, in Patai, *Messiah Texts*, pp. 31–32.

46. From Sofer, *Sippure Ya'akov*, pp. 35–36, in Patai, *Messiah Texts*, p. 32.

47. This issue is discussed in chap. 2.

48. The fourteenth-century rabbi and ethical philosopher Hasdai Crescas, a contemporary of rival popes Urban VI and Clement VII, takes up this matter with particular passion and acerbic humor. Among his arguments: had Jesus truly been the Messiah, peace and unity would reign, leaving no room for warring popes. In Sarachek, *Doctrine of the Messiah*, pp. 197–198.

49. While false messiahs are almost always viewed in a negative light, Irving Greenberg echoes Franz Rosenzweig with this different—and compelling—attitude: "Of course, every messianic movement so far has been proven to be premature (and caused many problems). Still the appearance of the movement shows that Judaism is alive and well," he states. "What a compliment to Judaism it is that our faith is still spawning would-be Messiahs—which it should be well and do until the real one comes." In Shalom Freedman and Irving Greenberg, *Living in the Image of God: Jewish Teachings to Perfect the World; Conversations with Rabbi Irving Greenberg* (Northvale, NJ: Jason Aronson, 1998), pp. 307–308.

50. In Leonard B. Gewirtz, *Jewish Spirituality: Hope and Redemption* (Hoboken, NJ: Ktav, 1986), p. 80. Other sources date his announcement to 1665 in Gaza; see *Encyclopaedia Judaica* (Jerusalem: Keter, 1971), 14:1224.

51. Quoted in *Encyclopaedia Judaica*, 14:1234.

52. This aspect of the Messiah is discussed fully in chap. 2.

53. Quoted in *Encyclopaedia Judaica*, 14:1223. The words are remindful of the tradition that "in the time to come all the animals which are unclean in this world God will declare to be clean," based on an intentionally variant reading of Psalm 146:7. See *Midrash Tehillim*

268a:4, in C. G. Montefiore and H. Loewe, eds., *A Rabbinic Anthology* (New York: Meridian Books; Philadelphia: Jewish Publication Society of America, 1963), p. 583.

54. Particularly in the form of the Frankists. These followers of eighteenth-century messianic pretender Jacob Frank, who proclaimed himself the reincarnation of Shabbatei Zevi, embraced the New Testament and practiced a bizarre amalgamation of Jewish, Christian, and sacrilegious customs before being baptized en masse as Catholics. However, the Church never fully accepted the sincerity of the Frankists' conversions and even imprisoned Frank for heresy.

55. Gewirtz, *Jewish Spirituality*, pp. 91ff.

56. The Schneerson phenomenon will be examined fully in chap. 6.

57. Cited by Harry James Cargas, in *Shadows of Auschwitz*, p. 161, in Joseph Telushkin, *Jewish Wisdom: Ethical, Spiritual, and Historical Lessons from the Great Works and Thinkers* (New York: William Morrow, 1994), p. 557.

CHAPTER TWO
The Messiah Will Rule Over Israel

1. From "*Me'al Pisgat Har HaTzofim,*" "From above the Peak of Mount Scopus," lyrics by Avigdor Hameiri, as excerpted in Chaim Stern, *Gates of Prayer: The New Union Prayerbook* (New York: Central Conference of American Rabbis, 1975), p. 611.

2. Aliyah is the Hebrew word for "ascending." "Making aliyah" means immigrating to Israel and also implies ascending to a higher or better place.

3. Charles W. Baughman, "Development of the Concept of the Messiah" (doctoral thesis, Hebrew Union College–Jewish Institute of Religion, 1959), pp. 7–10.

4. Although the Bible does not attest to the anointing of each and every king, according to Baughman "it seems most likely that every king, of both Israel and Judah, was thus anointed" (ibid., p. 27).

5. Ibid., p. 41.

6. Ibid., pp. 75–77. The historical and redemptive aspects of the shofar, a specially prepared ram's horn, are discussed further in chap. 5.

7. I do not include among them the mysterious unnamed "*mashiach* [or anointed one, who] will disappear and vanish" invoked in Daniel 9:26; although midrashic sources come to associate this figure with the Messiah ben Joseph, the context in which he arises is clearly apocalyptic rather than historical. See chap. 3. Nor do I include the also unnamed

hakohen hamashiach, "the anointed priest," who first appears in Leviticus 4:3; the designation is also used during post exilic times.

8. It is worth noting here that the role of even an explicitly anointed priest differs significantly from that of a messianic king. While "the anointing of the high priest consecrated him above all his brethren to God's service and gave him immediate access to God," a king's anointment "placed him in a special relationship to God, and established him as the one chosen by God to represent [God's] rulership in Israel and to bear witness to [God's] glory before the nations. As 'God's anointed one' the king was sacrosanct and inviolable"; Joseph Jacobs and Moses Buttenwieser, "Messiah," in *Jewish Encyclopedia,* www.jewishencyclopedia.com/articles/10729-messiah.

9. The identification of the non-Jewish Cyrus as a messiah may have influenced fourth-century-BCE Jews who appear to have embraced Alexander the Great as a messianic deliverer. See Jacobs and Buttenwieser, "Messiah."

10. Samson H. Levey, "The Messiah and the Messianic Era: Jewish and Christian Perspectives" (lecture for the Evangelical Theological Society, delivered at Hebrew Union College–Jewish Institutes of Religion, Los Angeles, 1970), p. 3. A compelling midrash that understands Isaiah 9's oracle "A child has been born to us" as a reference to Hezekiah states that God would have designated Hezekiah as the Messiah had Hezekiah only offered hymns of praise to God for the miracles wrought for him; Talmud, *Sanhedrin* 94a and *En Yaakov,* in H. N. Bialik and Y. H. Ravnitzky, eds., *The Book of Legends,* trans. William G. Braude (New York: Schocken Books, 1992), 138–139:165.

11. Joseph Klausner, *The Messianic Idea in Israel,* trans. W. F. Stinespring (New York: Macmillan, 1955), pp. 104–105.

12. Messianic longing marked even the time of Jewish sovereignty under the Maccabees and their descendants, known also as the Hasmoneans. Although not members of the House of David, the Hasmoneans had through military victory earned the right to govern the Land and lead the Jewish people. However, their lack of Davidic credentials, their combining the once-separate roles of political ruler and high priest, and particularly the Hasmonean ruler Aristobulus I's adopting the formal title "king" enraged many and sparked new literature that emphasized the primary importance of the Davidic Messiah.

13. Klausner, *Messianic Idea,* p. 16, with Levey, *Messiah and Messianic Era,* p. 2.

14. Levey, *Messiah and Messianic Era,* p. 2.

15. *Numbers Rabbah* 23:7, in Stern, *Gates of Prayer,* p. 603.

16. *Torah*, which literally means "teaching," refers to the first five books of the Bible: Genesis, Exodus, Leviticus, Numbers, and Deuteronomy. These are held especially sacred and traditionally viewed as given directly by God to Moses on Mount Sinai.

17. Edited and translated by T. Carmi in *Hebrew Verse*, pp. 348–349, as cited in Collette Sirat, *A History of Jewish Philosophy in the Middle Ages* (Cambridge: Cambridge University Press, 1985), p. 131.

18. In Abba Hillel Silver, *A History of Messianic Speculation in Israel* (Gloucester, MA: Peter Smith, 1978), p. 232.

19. This passage comes from the Pittsburgh Platform of 1885, the American Reform movement's first formal statement of principles. Later platforms would essentially repudiate the above quotation. The role of Israel in early Reform Judaism's messianic expectations is discussed fully in chap. 6.

20. The *Amidah*, which literally means "standing," is the central prayer in the Jewish worship service and is traditionally recited at least three times daily. The weekday *Amidah* comprises nineteen benedictions, several of which petition God for blessings associated with the Messianic Age.

21. *Pesikta deRav Kahana* 2:463–64, in Raphael Patai, *The Messiah Texts* (Detroit: Wayne State University, 1979), p. 185.

22. Rashi on Deuteronomy 30:3, cited in *Encyclopaedia Judaica* (Jerusalem: Keter, 1971), 8:1374.

23. As translated in Stern, *Gates of Prayer*, p. 765.

24. While the birth of the State of Israel may not in and of itself fulfill Jewish messianic hopes, S. Zeitlin convincingly holds that it was sufficiently redemptive to keep Jews from falling prey to false messiahs in the aftermath of the Holocaust; Leo Landman, ed., *Messianism in the Talmudic Era* (New York: Ktav, 1979), p. 513.

25. In Joseph Telushkin, *Jewish Wisdom: Ethical, Spiritual, and Historical Lessons from the Great Works and Thinkers* (New York: William Morrow, 1994), p. 605.

26. Adapted from ibid., p. 604.

27. In Leonard B. Gewirtz, *Jewish Spirituality: Hope and Redemption* (Hoboken, NJ: Ktav, 1986), pp. 83–84. This worldview motivated a number of Jews who settled in Jerusalem before the establishment of the State of Israel, believing that Jewish immigration to Zion would hasten the advent of the Messiah. And the philosophy endures, though more dangerously, today: At the extreme edge of the belief that the State of Israel is *resheit tz'michat ge'ulateinu* are members of the Third

Temple movement. Disregarded by mainstream Zionism and Judaism, this fringe group holds that Jewish sovereignty in the Land, the ingathering of the exiles, and the rebuilding of the Third Temple— by forcible means if necessary—must occur before the Messiah can be revealed. In a not dissimilar vein, Irving Greenberg attributes the "reckless political behavior" and "the growth of extremist solutions" among Israel's Gush Emunim to "runaway messianism." See Shalom Freedman and Irving Greenberg, *Living in the Image of God: Jewish Teachings to Perfect the World; Conversations with Rabbi Irving Greenberg* (Northvale, NJ: Jason Aronson, 1998), pp. 308–311.

28. *The Testament of Judah* in *Testament of the Twelve Tribes*, in Klausner, *Messianic Idea*, p. 316.

29. These are discussed fully in the section and the chapters that follow.

30. In Patai, *Messiah Texts*, pp. 272–273.

CHAPTER THREE
The Messiah Is a Warrior

1. Though Deuteronomy, relating Israelite history centuries before the birth of King David, does not of course speak of a messianic redeemer, the link between suffering and deliverance is clear and explicit.

2. Jerusalem Talmud, *Sotah* 9:15, cited in Ariel, *What Do Jews Believe? The Spiritual Foundations of Judaism* (New York: Schocken Books, 1995), pp. 224–225. I have rendered the translation gender inclusive.

3. Ibid.

4. Discovered by Bedouin shepherds in Wadi Qumran, near the Dead Sea, in 1947, the Dead Sea Scrolls offered a previously unimagined view into the Judaism of the Second Temple period. The Dead Sea Scrolls are likely the work of an ascetic, apocalyptic sect, who preserved in their writings not only the particular rules, customs, and beliefs of their community but also early versions of almost every book of the Hebrew Bible.

5. *Sefer Zerubbabel* literally means "The Book of Zerubbabel." Zerubbabel was a biblical figure, a descendant of King David who helped lead the Jews back to Jerusalem after the Babylonian Exile. He lived during the same time as the biblical prophets Haggai and Zechariah, who ascribed to him messianic significance.

6. *Sibylline Oracles* 3:796–807, excerpted, in Raphael Patai, *The Messiah Texts* (Detroit: Wayne State University Press, 1979), pp. 172–173.

7. *IV Ezra* 8:62–9:6, excerpted, in Joseph Klausner, *The Messianic Idea in Israel*, trans. W. F. Stinespring (New York: Macmillan, 1955), p. 353.

8. The Lower Galilee site of Arbael (or Arbela, known today as Arbel) is an important one. Second Temple–era Jews rebelling against Herod and the Roman occupation hid in Arbel's cliffs, and at least two significant messages of messianic consolation were delivered there. See chapter 1 and Zev Vilnay, *Legends of Palestine* (Philadelphia: Jewish Publication Society of America, 1932), p. 354. Hosea 10:14 also refers to a battle at Beit Arbel. Even in modern Israel, Arbel's legacy lives: a placard at Arbel National Park describes the apocalyptic battle foretold in *Sefer Zerubbabel* and relates the tradition that messianic redemption will begin in Arbel's valley.

9. Cited in and adapted from Martha Himmelfarb, "*Sefer Zerubbabel*," in *Rabbinic Fantasies*, ed. David Stern and Mark Jay Mirsky (New Haven: Yale University Press, 1990), p. 78.

10. A remarkable exception to this apocalyptic style and its messianic visions is the *Testament of Levi*, which portrays a priestly messiah— descended not from King David but from the House of Levi—whose work will be entirely spiritual and peaceful. Levi is, of course, the traditional ancestor of all priests in Israelite and Jewish tradition; Joseph Jacobs and Moses Buttenwieser, "Messiah," in *Jewish Encyclopedia*, www.jewishencyclopedia.com/articles/10729-messiah.

11. M. Friedlaender, cited in Klausner, *Messianic Idea*, p. 273.

12. In *Encyclopaedia Judaica* (Jerusalem: Keter, 1971) 7:691–693.

13. Literally, "The Book of Beliefs and Opinions." This tenth-century work—and its brilliant, influential author—attempted to use philosophy and rationalism to prove the truth of traditional Judaism.

14. In Himmelfarb, "*Sefer Zerubbabel*," pp. 80–81.

15. Ibid., p. 71.

16. Ibid., p. 75.

17. Ibid.

18. Not all depictions of multiple redeemers necessarily relate to these themes, as evidenced by some texts of the Dead Sea Scrolls and early apocalypses, but this tension does animate Judaism's most influential— and most fascinating—images of a second Messiah.

19. Although I use the name Messiah ben Joseph, sources refer to this figure as the Messiah ben Ephraim as well. Ephraim was the younger— though favored by his grandfather Jacob—son of Joseph; Joseph was the older son of Jacob's younger—and favored—wife Rachel.

20. While the lineage of the Messiah ben David obviously focuses on the paternal figure of David, legends surrounding the origin of the Messiah ben Joseph actually center on the maternal figure. According to the

midrash, God assuages the pain of Rachel's infertility by making her the mother of a Messiah (in Patai, *Messiah Texts*, p. 165). Other sources identify the son of the widow of Zarephath resurrected by Elijah as the Messiah ben Joseph; see 1 Kings 17:7–24, with Louis Ginzberg, *The Legends of the Jews*, vol. 6 (Philadelphia: Jewish Publication Society of America, 1959), p. 351. It is interesting to note that the emphasis of the maternal lineage of the Messiah ben Joseph parallels that given Mary, mother of Jesus, in Christian tradition.

21. The fifteenth-century sage Don Isaac Abravanel, an official in the Spanish king Ferdinand's court who went into exile after the expulsion of 1492, daringly but unconvincingly suggests that, intimidated by the stature and deeds of the Messiah ben Joseph, Christianity appropriated the figure and recast him as the Antichrist; Joseph Sarachek, *The Doctrine of the Messiah in Medieval Jewish Literature* (New York: Jewish Theological Society of America, 1932), pp. 262ff.

22. *IV Ezra* 7:27–30, in Patai, *Messiah Texts*, p. 167.

23. *Lekach Tov*, pp. 258–259, in Patai, *Messiah Texts*, pp. 169–170.

24. Controversial scholar Israel Knohl argues, in fact, that an earlier historical figure—a first-century-BCE Qumran leader and freedom fighter whom he identifies as "Menachem the Essene Messiah" and finds depicted in the Dead Sea Scrolls—inspired both the Messiah ben Joseph and the messianic character of Jesus.

25. Sarachek, *Doctrine of the Messiah*, p. 17.

26. Adapted from Himmelfarb, "*Sefer Zerubbabel*," p. 74. See also *Numbers Rabbah* 18:23, which states that every king in Jerusalem enjoyed possession of the staff and links its disappearance to the destruction of the Temple.

27. *Sefer Zerubbabel* gives the name Nehemiah son of Hushiel to the figure of the Messiah ben Joseph. "Nehemiah" can be translated as "God is my comfort."

28. *Sefer Zerubbabel* gives the name Menachem son of Amiel to the figure of the Messiah ben David. "Menachem," which derives from the same root as "Nehemiah" and means "comforter," is a name of messianic significance. The tradition that the Messiah will be descended from Hezekiah is a common one; scholars identify "Amiel" here as a reference to Hezekiah.

29. In Himmelfarb, "*Sefer Zerubbabel*," p. 74, and Patai, *Messiah Texts*, p. 126.

30. The number three is evocative in messianic as well as more general Jewish tradition; for example, as discussed in chapter 5, three shofar blasts will announce the culmination of the messianic redemption.

Another significant number in Judaism, seven, is also represented in apocalyptic literature; perhaps reflecting the biblical fall of Jericho after the Israelites had completed seven revolutions around the city, the Dead Sea Scrolls' *War Scroll* foretells the triumph of God and the Sons of Light after seven rounds of battle (columns 16–18, as displayed in the Shrine of the Book, Israel Museum, Jerusalem).

31. *B'reshit Rabbati*, pp. 130–131, in Patai, *Messiah Texts*, pp. 124–125.

32. Far more disturbing, however, is a similar legend that appears in the Jerusalem Talmud. In this account the Messiah's mother expresses her desire to "strangle my son ... for on the day he was born, the Temple was destroyed." Interestingly, this child too is called Menachem son of Hezekiah. In Israel Knohl, *The Messiah before Jesus: The Suffering Servant of the Dead Sea Scrolls*, trans. David Maisel (Berkeley: University of California Press, 2000), pp. 72–73.

33. *Zohar, Ra'aya Mehemna*, 3:67b–68a, in Patai, *Messiah Texts*, pp. 129–130.

34. Solomon Buber's note to *Midrash Mishlei*, Buber ed., p. 87, in Patai, *Messiah Texts*, p. 22.

35. In Edwin Cole Goldberg, "Book of Zerubbabel," rabbinic thesis, Hebrew Union College–Jewish Institute of Religion, 1989), p. 40.

36. *Zohar* 2:132a, in Patai, *Messiah Texts*, p. 195.

37. In Klausner, *Messianic Idea*, p. 360.

38. In Himmelfarb, "*Sefer Zerubbabel*," p. 78. The inspiration for this passage is Isaiah 11:4, which prophesies that the heir of the House of David shall "slay the wicked with the breath of his lips."

39. Gershom Scholem, *The Messianic Idea in Judaism* (London: George Allen & Unwin, 1971), p. 18.

40. *Yalkut Shimoni, Vayishlach*, in Patai, *Messiah Texts*, p. 139.

41. In Patai, *Messiah Texts*, p. 316; italics mine.

42. Babylonian Talmud, *Megillah* 17b; in Ephraim E. Urbach, *The Sages: Their Concepts and Beliefs*, trans. Israel Abrahams (Jerusalem: Magnes Press, 1987), p. 655.

CHAPTER FOUR

The Messiah Will Change Everything

1. Talmud, *Ketubot* 111b, in Joseph Klausner, *The Messianic Idea in Israel*, trans. W. F. Stinespring (New York: Macmillan, 1955), pp. 409–410.

2. Jerusalem Talmud, *Shekalim* 50a, in Raphael Patai, *The Messiah Texts* (Detroit: Wayne State University, 1979), pp. 231–232.

3. Talmud, *Ketubot* 111b, in Patai, *Messiah Texts*, pp. 232–233.

4. Ibid.

5. *Pirkei Mashiach*, BhM 3:77–78, in Patai, *Messiah Texts*, pp. 233–234.

6. *Sifra, Behukotai*, chap. 3, in Klausner, *Messianic Idea*, p. 511.

7. In Charles Chavel, trans., *Ramban Commentary: Leviticus* (New York: Shiloh, 1974), pp. 456–457.

8. *Sifra, Behukotai* 2:1; *Yalkut haMakhiri*, p. 86, in Patai, *Messiah Texts*, p. 259.

9. Gershom Scholem, *Major Trends in Jewish Mysticism* (New York: Schocken Books, 1941), p. 224.

10. Quoted in Gershom Scholem, *The Messianic Idea in Judaism* (London: George Allen & Unwin, 1971), pp. 28–29.

11. Talmud, *Bava Batra* 75a and *Sanhedrin* 100a, in Klausner, *Messianic Idea*, p. 510.

12. *Zohar* 1:113b, *Midrash HaNe'elam*, in Patai, *Messiah Texts*, p. 263.

13. *Exodus Rabbah* 15:21, in Patai, *Messiah Texts*, pp. 260–261.

14. Talmud, *Berachot* 17a.

15. *Pirkei Mashiach*, BhM 3:77–78, in Patai, *Messiah Texts*, pp. 233–234.

16. *Mechilta, Bachodesh*, chap. 2, in Klausner, *Messianic Idea*, p. 512.

17. From *Yad HaHazakah, Shofetim, Hilchot Melachim* 11–12, in Patai, *Messiah Texts*, p. 325.

18. *Zohar* 1:113b, *Midrash HaNe'elam*, in Patai, *Messiah Texts*, p. 263.

19. From *Yad HaHazakah, Shofetim, Hilchot Melachim* 11–12, in Patai, *Messiah Texts*, pp. 325–326.

20. *Sifra, Behukotai*, chap. 3, in Klausner, *Messianic Idea*, p. 511.

21. Talmud, *Bava Batra* 122a, in Klausner, *Messianic Idea*, p. 511.

22. *Midrash Tanchuma, Noach*, paragraph 19, in Patai, *Messiah Texts*, p. 260.

23. *Midrash vaYosha*, BhM 1:55, in Patai, *Messiah Texts*, p. 261.

24. *Leviticus Rabbah* 9:7, in Scholem, *Messianic Idea*, p. 54.

25. *Yalkut* and *Midrash Mishlei* to Proverbs 9:2, in Scholem, *Messianic Idea*, pp. 54–55. See also Jerusalem Talmud, *Megillah* 1:5.

26. Yom Kippur, the Day of Atonement, mandates fasting and refraining from enjoyable activities; Passover enjoins us to eat only foods containing no leaven.

27. The Purim story also reflects another paradigm of Jewish redemption, recounting the conflict between Haman, the descendant of Israel's ancient enemy Amalek, and Mordechai and Esther, descendants of the tribe of Benjamin who act as God's agents in bringing Haman's defeat. See Elaine Rose Glickman, *Haman and the*

Jews: A Portrait from Rabbinic Literature (Northvale, NJ: Jason Aronson, 1999), chap. 2 and 6.

28. In Klausner, *Messianic Idea*, p. 500.

29. In Martha Himmelfarb, "*Sefer Zerubbabel*," in *Rabbinic Fantasies*, ed. David Stern and Mark Jay Mirsky (New Haven: Yale University Press, 1990), p. 79.

30. David G. Roskies, *Against the Apocalypse: Responses to Catastrophe in Modern Jewish Culture* (Cambridge, MA: Harvard University Press, 1984), pp. 38–39.

31. Abraham Joshua Heschel, perhaps the most celebrated theologian of modern times, boldly describes the grandeur of this new Torah: "The Torah ... could not exist or be fulfilled in its perfect form in a world which is stained with imperfections.... The Torah which [one] learns in this world is *vanity* in comparison with the Torah [which will be learned in the days] of the Messiah"; in Abraham Joshua Heschel, *God in Search of Man: A Philosophy of Judaism* (New York: Noonday Press, 1955), pp. 263–264. The latter half of his statement cites the midrashic collection *Ecclesiastes Rabbah* and recalls the *Zohar*'s characterization of the Torah of the Messianic Age; italics are his.

32. Adapted from Patai, *Messiah Texts*, pp. 256–257.

33. Rabbi Alexandri in *Genesis Rabbah* 78:1, in H. N. Bialik and Y. N. Ravnitzky, eds., *The Book of Legends*, trans. William G. Braude (New York: Schocken Books, 1992), 401:18.

34. Rabbi Jeremiah in the Jerusalem Talmud, *Kilayim* 9:3, 32b, and *Genesis Rabbah* 100:2, in Bialik and Ravnitzky, *Book of Legends*, 402:25.

35. Some of this distress may be mitigated, however, by the *Messianic Apocalypse*, a text contained in the Dead Sea Scrolls that suggests pre-Christian belief in a healing, resurrecting Messiah; in Geoffrey W. Dennis, *The Encyclopedia of Jewish Myth, Magic and Mysticism* (Woodbury, MN: Llewellyn, 2007), p. 170.

36. See, for example, C. G. Montefiore and H. Loewe, eds., *A Rabbinic Anthology* (New York: Meridian Books; Philadelphia: Jewish Publication Society of America, 1963), p. 600.

37. Genesis 22:17, among others.

38. Adapted from Talmud, *Ketubot* 111b, in Patai, *Messiah Texts*, p. 199.

39. In Louis Jacobs, *A Jewish Theology* (West Orange, NJ: Behrman House, 1973), p. 311, and Joseph Sarachek, *The Doctrine of the Messiah in Medieval Jewish Literature* (New York: Jewish Theological Society of America, 1932), p. 47.

40. In order to keep the physical body as united as possible in preparation for resurrection.

41. It is worth noting that the midrash credits Isaac with composing the *chatimah*, or conclusion, of this blessing upon his own resurrection from death. A compelling tradition holds that Abraham actually completed the sacrifice of Isaac on Mount Moriah, but Isaac was revived by a heavenly voice. Restored, Isaac praised God as "Resurrector of the dead." See Genesis 22 with Louis Ginzberg, *The Legends of the Jews*, vol. 1, trans. Henrietta Szold (Philadelphia: Jewish Publication Society of America, 1939), pp. 281ff. Interestingly, the ram sacrificed in place of Isaac (Genesis 22:13) will also make an appearance at the resurrection of the dead: according to *Pirkei deRabbi Eliezer*, chap. 31, the sinews of the ram were used to craft the strings of David's harp (e.g., 1 Samuel 16:23), and David himself will play this harp as the dead return to life; see Dennis, *Encyclopedia of Jewish Myth*, p. 115.

42. This aspect of the resurrection of the dead is, admittedly, diminished by a philosophical tradition that the physical revival is only temporary, a sort of way station for "the souls of the righteous [who] will ascend to the luminous region, the 'world to come'"; Sarachek, *Doctrine of the Messiah*, p. 125, on the esteemed twelfth-century sage Abraham ibn Ezra and Maimonides. The World to Come is discussed further in chap. 5.

43. In *S'udat Livyatan*, BhM 6:150–151, in Patai, *Messiah Texts*, p. 240.

44. *Alphabet of Rabbi Akiva*, BhM 3:33–34, in Patai, *Messiah Texts*, pp. 242–243. All the following citations in this paragraph are from this text.

45. *Numbers Rabbah* 13:2, in Patai, *Messiah Texts*, pp. 237–238.

46. *Alphabet of Rabbi Akiva*, BhM 3:33–34, in Patai, *Messiah Texts*, pp. 242–243. *Song of Songs Rabbah* 1:3/3 describes a "choir of the righteous" comprising "righteous on this side and righteous on this side, and the Holy One, blessed be God, in the center; and they will dance before God with zest."

47. *Numbers Rabbah* 13:2, in Patai, *Messiah Texts*, pp. 237–238.

48. Talmud, *Bava Batra* 74b–75a, in Patai, *Messiah Texts*, pp. 236–237.

49. *Pirkei deRabbi Eliezer*, chap. 10, and *Midrash Jonah* in Eisenstein, pp. 218–19, in Bialik and Ravnitzky, *Book of Legends*, 133–134:142.

50. *Nistarot Rabbi Shimon bar Yochai*, BhM 3:80, in Patai, *Messiah Texts*, p. 238.

51. *Leviticus Rabbah* 13:3.

52. *Pirkei Mashiach*, BhM 3:76–77, in Patai, *Messiah Texts*, pp. 239–240.

CHAPTER FIVE

The Messiah Will Establish God's Dominion

1. *The Assumption of Moses* 10:1–10, excerpted and adapted from Joseph Klausner, *The Messianic Idea in Israel*, trans. W. F. Stinespring (New York: Macmillan, 1955), pp. 327–328.

2. Italics mine.

3. Moshe Idel notes a few fascinating exceptions to this rule—including a Talmudic passage that calls the Messiah by God's Ineffable Name—and insight into their origin and significance. See Moshe Idel, *Messianic Mystics* (New Haven: Yale University Press, 1998), pp. 22ff.

4. *Olam Haba*, the World to Come, is an essential yet ambiguous term in Jewish thought, associated with both an individual's afterlife and the greater messianic redemption. The distinction made between *Yamot HaMashiach* and the more mysterious *Olam Haba* is perhaps best summarized by Rabbi Yochanan in the Talmud, *Berachot* 34b: "Every prophet prophesied only for the days of the Messiah; but as for the world to come, no eye has seen what God has prepared"; in C. G. Montefiore and H. Loewe, *A Rabbinic Anthology* (New York: Meridian Books; Philadelphia: Jewish Publication Society of America, 1963), p. 598. Particularly among medieval sages, *Olam Haba* was also envisioned as a purely spiritual realm.

5. For a full account of Elijah's life and deeds, see 1 Kings 17–2 Kings 2.

6. The image of Elijah's chariot—*merkavah* in Hebrew—is among the most famous and enduring in biblical literature. Three striking examples: an entire genre of mystical literature that bears the name *Ma'aseh Merkavah*, "the Work [Inspired by] the Chariot"; the Oscar-winning film *Chariots of Fire*, and the modern Israeli tank, called in Hebrew *merkavah*.

7. Just how lasting and meaningful is this aspect of Elijah struck me during my year of rabbinical training in Jerusalem. On a cold wet night, one of my classmates took off his raincoat and offered it to an older gentleman sitting along the road. The man ran after my classmate, calling, "*Atah hu Eliyahu hanavi?*" "Are you Elijah the prophet?"

8. In Barbara Diamond Goldin, *Journeys with Elijah: Eight Tales of the Prophet* (San Diego: Gulliver Books, 1999), p. 10.

9. *Ecclesiastes Rabbah* 4:1, in Raphael Patai, *The Messiah Texts* (Detroit: Wayne State University, 1979), p. 142.

10. *Pesikta Rabbati, piskas* 35–37, and *Yalkut*, Isaiah 499, excerpted, in H. N. Bialik and Y. H. Ravnitzky, eds., *The Book of Legends*, trans. William G. Braude (New York: Schocken Books, 1992), 395–397:56.

11. Literally meaning "separation," *Havdalah* is a brief ceremony that formally concludes the Sabbath and begins a new week.

12. *Song of Songs Rabbah* 2:13/4, in *Encyclopaedia Judaica* (Jerusalem: Keter, 1971), 6:637.

13. *Genesis Rabbah* 7:19, in *Encyclopaedia Judaica*, 6:637.

14. *Mishnah Eduyyot* 8:7, in Klausner, *Messianic Idea*, pp. 453–454.

15. *Mishnah Sotah* 9:15, in Patai, *Messiah Texts*, p. 143. Elijah's place in the resurrection of the dead hearkens to one of his first deeds as God's prophet: resurrecting the dead child of a widow who had given him food and shelter (1 Kings 17:17–24). Chapter 3 examines in further detail the significance of the resurrected boy.

16. *Mechilta deRabbi Ishmael*, p. 80, in Patai, *Messiah Texts*, pp. 142–143.

17. *Pesikta Rabbati*, *piskas* 35-37, and *Yalkut*, Isaiah 499, excerpted, in Bialik and Ravnitzky, *Book of Legends*, 395–397:56.

18. *Pirkei deRabbi Eliezer*, chap. 31, in Louis Ginzberg, *The Legends of the Jews*, vol. 1, trans. Henrietta Szold (Philadelphia: Jewish Publication Society of America, 1939), p. 284.

19. *Tefillat Rabbi Shimon bar Yochai*, BhM 4:124–126, in Patai, *Messiah Texts*, pp. 157–159.

20. *Ma'asei Daniel*, pp. 225–226, excerpted and adapted, in Patai, *Messiah Texts*, pp. 143–144.

21. The plural of *shofar*.

22. Maimonides, *Mishneh Torah*, *Hilchot Teshuvah* 3:4, excerpted from Chaim Stern, ed., *Gates of Repentance: The New Union Prayerbook for the Days of Awe* (New York: Central Conference of American Rabbis, 1984), p. 139.

23. *Tanchuma Buber* 1:115, and others, in Ginzberg, *Legends of the Jews*, vol. 1, p. 285.

24. In Stern, *Gates of Repentance*, p. 215.

25. *Midrash Mishlei*, Buber ed., p. 87, in Patai, *Messiah Texts*, p. 22.

26. While the lengthy and often conflicting midrashic lists of individuals excluded from the life of the World to Come—from deniers of the scriptural basis for the resurrection of the dead to the biblical kings Jeroboam, Ahab, and Manasseh—stand as obvious exceptions, these traditions are concerned more with polemics than with a comprehensive depiction of divine judgment and justice. So too the teaching of the School of Shammai that humanity will be divided into three classes of people—"perfectly righteous," "perfectly wicked," and

"intermediates"—on the Day of Judgment and treated accordingly. See Montefiore and Loewe, *Rabbinic Anthology*, pp. 601ff.

27. Talmud, *Sanhedrin* 91a–b, in Patai, *Messiah Texts*, p. 219.

28. *Alphabet of Rabbi Akiva*, BhM 3:27–29, excerpted, in Patai, *Messiah Texts*, pp. 252–253.

29. *Midrash Hallel*, BhM 5:107, in Patai, *Messiah Texts*, pp. 218–219.

30. It is essential to state, however, that gentiles are not consigned to punishment simply because of their religious beliefs. As C. G. Montefiore and H. Loewe note, "The view of [Talmudic sage] R. Joshua that the righteous of all nations (that is, of all non-Jews) would inherit the world to come became the accepted doctrine of the Synagogue" (*Rabbinic Anthology*, p. 582).

31. *Pesikta Rabbati, piskas* 35–37, and *Yalkut*, Isaiah 499, excerpted, in Bialik and Ravnitzky, *Book of Legends*, 395–397:56.

32. *1 Enoch* 62:10–13, excerpted, in Patai, *Messiah Texts*, pp. 212–213.

33. *Exodus Rabbah* 7:4, in Montefiore and Loewe, *Rabbinic Anthology*, p. 589.

34. *Pesikta Rabbati, piskas* 35–37, and *Yalkut*, Isaiah 499, excerpted, in Bialik and Ravnitzky, *Book of Legends*, 395–397:56. The nations' acclaim comes from Psalm 144:15.

35. While not all of the biblical prophets envision such a peaceful and joyous process (Zechariah is an obvious and unsettling exception) the pervasive sense of reconciliation and unity is striking and was for our sages clearly inspirational.

36. *Avot deRabbi Natan*, chap. 35, in Kochan, ed. by Cohen and Mendes-Flohr, p. 1035.

37. *Midrash Tanchuma, Noach*, paragraph 19, in Patai, *Messiah Texts*, p. 260.

38. In Gershom Scholem, *The Messianic Idea in Judaism* (London: George Allen & Unwin, 1971), p. 40. This teaching is especially interesting when juxtaposed with an earlier midrashic tradition that "at that hour will God brighten the light of King Messiah and of Israel, so that all the nations who are in darkness and in gloom, will walk in the light of the Messiah and of Israel"; *Pesikta Rabbati* 162a–162b, in Montefiore and Loewe, *Rabbinic Anthology*, pp. 606–607.

39. In Idel, *Messianic Mystics*, p. 61.

40. Account of messianic dream of Hayyim Vital, a sixteenth-century student of Isaac Luria and a self-proclaimed redeemer, as related and interpreted in Idel, *Messianic Myths*, p. 168.

41. The invocation of "O peoples" and "O nations" appears in variant manuscripts and resonates with the passage's universal tone.

42. Charles W. Baughman, "Development of the Concept of the Messiah" (doctoral thesis, Hebrew Union College–Jewish Institute of Religion, 1959), p. 128. I have taken the liberty of excising gender references from his work and rendering his reference to God as "the Eternal."

43. Ezekiel 40:5–47:12 contains comprehensive instructions for rebuilding the Temple; although the text may appear a blueprint for a real-life reconstruction of the Temple, it is actually utopian—or messianic—in nature.

44. *Pirkei Mashiach*, BhM 3:74–75, in Patai, *Messiah Texts*, pp. 226–227.

45. Even today, traditional Jews pray three times a day for this literal restoration. Among the benedictions of the *Amidah* are these words: "Restore the sacrificial service to the Holy of Holies in Your sanctuary, and the fire-offerings of Israel."

46. Moses Maimonides, in *Yad HaHazakah, Shofetim, Hilchot Melachim* 11–12, in Scholem, *Messianic Idea*, p. 29. Interestingly, Don Isaac Abravanel—who disagrees with Maimonides on many significant issues—echoes this theme, describing as the soul's reward in the World to Come a true understanding of God's nature; in Philip Birnbaum, *A Book of Jewish Concepts* (New York: Hebrew Publishing Co., 1964), p. 461.

47. Maimonides, in *Yad HaHazakah, Shofetim, Hilchot Melachim* 11–12, in Scholem, *Messianic Idea*, p. 29. This theme also appears in the work of other thinkers, perhaps most intriguingly Rabbi Shneour Zalman of Lyady, the founder of Chabad Hasidism.

48. Scholem, *Messianic Idea*, pp. 70, 40.

49. Though the theme of individual salvation would become associated primarily with mysticism—and rightfully so—it would recur in twentieth-century Jewish existentialist philosophy with Franz Rosenzweig, who taught that discovering and fulfilling the reason for our creation is an essential aspect of redemption.

50. In 1492 Spain expelled her Jews, a trauma of widespread and enduring magnitude that directly and indirectly reshaped mystical messianic belief. It is also important to note that the teachings cited here were not universally held; the *Zohar*, for example, speaks of a communal and supernatural redemption.

51. Scholem, *Messianic Idea*, p. 39. I have retained the masculine language because at the time of which Scholem speaks, Kabbalah was the exclusive domain of men.

52. *Sefer Toldot Adam*, in Idel, *Messianic Mystics*, p. 78.

53. Idel, *Messianic Mystics*, p. 78.

54. The term *tikkun olam*, "repairing the world" is an ancient one, originating in the Mishnah and a contemporaneous legal collection known as the *Tosefta*. Although in modern times *tikkun olam* often signifies acts of charity and social justice, the phrase arguably became most famous in its association with mysticism, in the context of gathering shards of divine light. Even today many people who interpret *tikkun olam* as a call for social action envision themselves as symbolically gathering these shards—healing the brokenness in our society and repairing our world.

55. Idel, *Messianic Mystics*, p. 223.

56. Ibid.

57. Scholem, *Messianic Idea*, p. 47.

CHAPTER SIX
The Messiah Is Us

1. Often mistranslated as "charity," *tzedakah* actually means "justice." The term underscores the Jewish tenet that giving *tzedakah*—that is, helping those who are in need—is a strict religious obligation.

2. Although the parallels with Christianity's beliefs about Jesus are obvious, Jewish tradition completely rejects this association. The teachings of Abraham ibn Ezra and Moses ben Nachman (Nachmanides) on the subject are particularly compelling; see Joseph Sarachek, *The Doctrine of the Messiah in Medieval Jewish Literature* (New York: Jewish Theological Society of America, 1932), pp. 116, 170–171.

3. While this communal identification is indeed the dominant interpretation of the suffering servant, it is worth noting that the theme of an individual suffering messiah is not foreign to Judaism. Examples include early-twenty-first-century scholarship on "Gabriel's Revelation"—a likely first-century-BCE apocalyptic text inscribed on a stone tablet recovered near the Dead Sea, which describes a suffering and possibly resurrected messiah—as well as the theories of Israel Knohl and, of course, the enduring figure of the Messiah ben Joseph.

4. *Pesikta Rabbati*, *piskas* 35–37, and *Yalkut*, Isaiah 499, excerpted, in H. N. Bialik and Y. H. Ravnitzky, eds., *The Book of Legends*, trans. William G. Braude (New York: Schocken Books, 1992), 395–397:56. See also C. G. Montefiore and H. Loewe, eds. *A Rabbinic Anthology* (New York: Meridian Books; Philadelphia: Jewish Publication Society of America, 1963), pp. 584–586. Strikingly, God calls the Messiah in these passages Ephraim, reminiscent of the appellation Messiah ben Ephraim, a name used interchangeably with the suffering Messiah ben Joseph. Although

the text depicts the Messiah's suffering for the sins of Israel, the parallel with Israel's suffering for the sake of redemption is clear.

5. Moshe Idel, *Messianic Mystics* (New Haven: Yale University Press, 1998), pp. 212ff. especially p. 241.

6. Gershom Scholem, *The Messianic Idea in Judaism* (London: George Allen & Unwin, 1971), p. 200.

7. As revealed in an encounter between the Besht and the Messiah, as related in a letter attributed to the Besht, cited in Elie Wiesel, *Souls on Fire: Portraits and Legends of Hasidic Masters* (New York: Simon & Schuster, 1982), p. 24.

8. Leo Baeck, *This People Israel: The Meaning of Jewish Existence*, trans. Albert H. Friedlander (Philadelphia: Jewish Publication Society of America, 1965), p. 331.

9. Martin Buber, *Tales of the Hasidim* (New York: Schocken Books, 1947), p. 4.

10. Martin Buber prefers to render *tzaddikim* as "those who stood the test" or "the proven." Ibid., p. 1.

11. Ibid., pp. 283–284.

12. Ibid., pp. 103–104.

13. Ibid., pp. 148, 267–268.

14. Before the rise of Hitler, an entire branch of Hasidism was known as Chabad. Founded by Rabbi Shneour Zalman of Lyady in Belorussia at the end of the nineteenth century, the Chabad movement advanced the importance of study and intellectualism alongside emotion in the service of God; the name itself—an acronym for *Chochmah, Binah, v'Dayat*, "Wisdom, Understanding, and Knowledge"—attests to Chabad's character. The Lubavitch school—which took its name from Lubavitch, its town of origin—was the only Chabad sect that survived the Holocaust. For this tragic reason, the names "Chabad" and "Lubavitch" can be used interchangeably today.

15. Chabad-Lubavitchers refer to these emissaries as *shluchim*.

16. Chabad-Lubavitchers generally refer to the Messiah as *Moshiach*.

17. Among the most prominent—and most vehement—critics on this point is Yeshiva University's head of Jewish studies, Professor David Berger. See especially his book *The Rebbe, the Messiah, and the Scandal of Orthodox Indifference* (London: Littman Library of Jewish Civilization, 2001).

18. In the March/April 2012 issue of *Moment*, Rabbi Shlomo Ezagui, head of the Chabad House in North Palm Beach, Florida, stated, "I believe that the Lubavitcher rebbe, Rabbi Schneerson, is the *mashiach*.... The *mashiach* can come from the dead.... The rebbe's death shook up a lot

of people, and not everyone was able to resolve their questions and move on with greater faith." See p. 33.

19. See, e.g., the foreword to *Please Tell Me What the Rebbe Said*, a children's book edited by Malka Touger and advertised on Chabad's official website, Chabad.org.

20. In Jim Yardley, "Messianic Fervor for Late Rabbi Divides Many Lubavitchers," *New York Times*, June 29, 1998.

21. This early Reform Judaism is now called classical Reform, and its originators classical Reformers.

22. While a human-driven redemption may appear remindful of mystical tradition, scholar Moshe Idel holds that classical Reform's messianic views are not rooted in Kabbalah. See Idel, *Messianic Mystics*, 173–174. Indeed, these ideas are far more completely reflected in the universalist, anti-Zionist teachings of influential mid-nineteenth- and early-twentieth-century German Jewish philosopher Hermann Cohen.

23. German Reformer Samuel Holdheim even invoked this supposedly emerging redemption to justify some of his most radical proposals. Arguing that "the dawn of the messianic era" had already arrived in the form of Emancipation, he cited the Talmud's assertion that "ceremonial law" would not apply in the World to Come and called for the immediate elimination of kashrut, ritual garb such as tallit and tefillin, Sabbath restrictions, and the like; in *Encyclopaedia Judaica* (Jerusalem: Keter, 1971) 14:25–26.

24. In *Encyclopaedia Judaica*, 14:26.

25. Because of its longer history and more radical expressions of liturgy and theology, Reform Judaism remains the focus of this discussion. Conservative Judaism, however, yields a similarly vague position on redemption, defining as the "thrust" of "Jewish eschatological thinking" a conviction that "in partnership with God, we can create an ever more perfect social order—not inevitably, not steadily, and perhaps not in our lifetimes—but eventually" and concluding simply that "we do not know when the Messiah will come, nor whether he will be a charismatic human figure or is a symbol of the redemption of humankind from the evils of the world"; from *"Emet ve'Emunah"* (literally, "Truth and Faith"), Conservative Judaism's 1998 statement of principles. Interestingly, not even Orthodoxy has completely resolved the crisis of modern Jewish messianism; although the movement officially upholds the traditional messianic expectations described by Maimonides, prominent Orthodox scholar Steven T. Katz has acknowledged, "Almost all Jews today ... don't discuss it. That is true

even of the modern Orthodox," in Joshua O. Haberman, *The God I Believe In* (New York: Free Press, 1994), p. 90.

26. Elyse Frishman, ed., *Mishkan T'filah: A Reform Siddur* (New York: Central Conference of America Rabbis, 2007), p. 589.

27. Ibid., p. 588.

28. In "Columbus Platform: The Guiding Principles of Reform Judaism," adopted by the Central Conference of American Rabbis in 1937, during the early years of Nazism.

29. In "A Statement of Principles for Reform Judaism," adopted by the Central Conference of American Rabbis, in Pittsburgh, Pennsylvania, in 1999.

30. Arthur Green, *Seek My Face: A Jewish Mystical Theology* (Woodstock, VT: Jewish Lights, 2003), pp. 179, 180.

31. Robert N. Levine, *There Is No Messiah and You're It* (Woodstock, VT: Jewish Lights, 2003), pp. 13–14.

32. Abraham Joshua Heschel, *God in Search of Man: A Philosophy of Judaism* (New York: Noonday Press, 1955), p. 379; italics mine. Reform theologian Eugene B. Borowitz echoes this theme—and shall perhaps inspire a new liberal messianic vision—in "A Jewish Theology of Social Action," *CCAR Journal*, Spring 2008.

33. The website of the Kabbalah Centre, www.kabbalah.com.

34. Sylvia Boorstein, *That's Funny, You Don't Look Buddhist: On Being a Faithful Jew and a Passionate Buddhist* (New York: HarperCollins, 1998), p. 5.

35. Adapted from Frishman, *Mishkan T'filah*, pp. 138–139.

36. Talmud, *Shabbat* 31a.

37. In Haberman, *God I Believe In*, p. 56.

38. *Kristallnacht*, or Night of the Broken Glass, refers to the devastating Nazi-organized outbreak of violence against the Jews of Germany on November 9, 1938.

Author's Note

1. According to Jewish legend, God spoke these words before healing all sick and wounded Israelites in preparation for the Revelation at Mount Sinai. This act, of course, foretells the messianic restoration to wholeness and peace. In Louis Ginzberg, *The Legends of the Jews*, vol. 3, trans. Paul Radin (Philadelphia: Jewish Publication Society of America, 1954), p. 78.

2. In Edwin Cole Goldberg, "Book of Zerubbabel" (rabbinic thesis, Hebrew Union College–Jewish Institute of Religion, 1989), p. 33.

Amen—which comes from the Hebrew root meaning "belief" or "faith"—and *selah*—which appears to serve in the book of Psalms as a note for musicians or readers reciting the text but can also connote "forever" or "eternity"—are traditional concluding words for Jewish prayers.

SUGGESTIONS FOR FURTHER READING

Abrams, Judith Z. *The Other Talmud—The Yerushalmi: Unlocking the Secrets of The Talmud of Israel for Judaism Today.* Woodstock, VT: Jewish Lights Publishing, 2012.

Ariel, David S. *What Do Jews Believe? The Spiritual Foundations of Judaism.* New York: Schocken Books, 1995.

Baeck, Leo. *This People Israel: The Meaning of Jewish Existence.* Translated by Albert H. Friedlander. Philadelphia: Jewish Publication Society of America, 1965.

Baughman, Charles W. "Development of the Concept of the Messiah." Doctoral thesis, Hebrew Union College–Jewish Institute of Religion, 1959.

Berger, Joseph. "A Place All Their Own in the Jewish Kaleidoscope." *Jewish Daily Forward,* June 6, 2003.

Bialik, H. N., and Y. H. Ravnitzky, eds. *The Book of Legends.* Translated by William G. Braude. New York: Schocken Books, 1992.

Birnbaum, Philip. *A Book of Jewish Concepts.* New York: Hebrew Publishing Company, 1964.

Boorstein, Sylvia. *That's Funny, You Don't Look Buddhist: On Being a Faithful Jew and a Passionate Buddhist.* New York: HarperCollins, 1998.

Borowitz, Eugene B. "A Jewish Theology of Social Action." *CCAR Journal,* Spring 2008.

Bronner, Ethan. "Ancient Tablet Ignites Debate on Messiah and Resurrection." *New York Times,* July 6, 2008.

Bruni, Frank. "To Some, Messiah Is the Message: Media Campaign for Late Rabbi Divides Lubavitch Movement." *New York Times,* February 25, 1996.

Buber, Martin. *Tales of the Hasidim.* New York: Schocken Books, 1947.

Camus, Albert. *Caligula and Three Other Plays.* Translated by Stuart Gilbert. New York: Vintage Books, 1958.

Chavel, Charles, trans. *Ramban Commentary: Leviticus.* New York: Shiloh Publishing House, 1974.

Cohn-Sherbok, Dan. *The Jewish Messiah.* London: T&T Clark International, 2000.

Danby, Herbert, trans. *The Mishnah.* New York: Oxford University Press, 1933.

Davis, Avrohom, trans. and anthologizer. *The Complete Metsudah Siddur.* Brooklyn: Metsudah Publications, 1990.

Dennis, Geoffrey W. *The Encyclopedia of Jewish Myth, Magic and Mysticism.* Woodbury, MN: Llewellyn Publications, 2007.

Donin, Hayim Halevy. *To Be a Jew: A Guide to Jewish Observance in Contemporary Life.* New York: Basic Books, 1972.

Encyclopaedia Judaica. Jerusalem: Keter Publishing House, 1971.

Epstein, I., ed. *The Babylonian Talmud.* London: Soncino Press, 1960.

Feld, Edward. *The Spirit of Renewal: Crisis and Response in Jewish Life.* Woodstock, VT: Jewish Lights Publishing, 1991.

Fishkoff, Sue. "Matisyahu Dishes Out Torah, Even Dating Tips at Jewlicious." Jewish Telegraphic Agency, March 4, 2008.

Fishkoff, Sue. *The Rebbe's Army: Inside the World of Chabad-Lubavitch.* New York: Schocken Books, 2003.

Freedman, H., and Maurice Simon, eds. *The Midrash Rabbah.* London: Soncino Press, 1977.

Freedman, Shalom, and Irving Greenberg. *Living in the Image of God: Jewish Teachings to Perfect the World: Conversations with Rabbi Irving Greenberg.* Northvale, NJ: Jason Aronson, 1998.

Frishman, Elyse, ed. *Mishkan T'filah: A Reform Siddur.* New York: Central Conference of American Rabbis, 2007.

Gewirtz, Leonard B. *Jewish Spirituality: Hope and Redemption.* Hoboken, NJ: Ktav, 1986.

Gillman, Neil. *The Death of Death: Resurrection and Immortality in Jewish Thought.* Woodstock, VT: Jewish Lights Publishing, 2000.

Ginzberg, Louis. *The Legends of the Jews.* Vol. 1. Translated by Henrietta Szold. Philadelphia: Jewish Publication Society of America, 1939.

Ginzberg, Louis. *The Legends of the Jews.* Vol. 3. Translated by Paul Radin. Philadelphia: Jewish Publication Society of America, 1954.

Ginzberg, Louis. *The Legends of the Jews.* Vol. 6. Philadelphia: Jewish Publication Society of America, 1959.

Glickman, Elaine Rose. *Haman and the Jews: A Portrait from Rabbinic Literature.* Northvale, NJ: Jason Aronson, 1999.

Goldberg, Edwin Cole. *Book of Zerubbabel.* Rabbinic thesis, Hebrew Union College–Jewish Institute of Religion, 1989.

Goldin, Barbara Diamond. *Journeys with Elijah: Eight Tales of the Prophet.* San Diego: Gulliver Books, 1999.

Goldman, Ari L. "Debate Splits Lubavitcher Hasidim: Showdown Nears on Whether Grand Rebbe Is the Messiah." *New York Times,* January 29, 1993.

Goldman, Ari L. "Rabbi Schneerson Led a Small Hasidic Sect to World Prominence." *New York Times,* June 13, 1994.

Gonzalez, David. "Rebbe Leaves All to Group and Doesn't Pick Successor." *New York Times,* June 15, 1994.

Green, Arthur. *Seek My Face: A Jewish Mystical Theology.* Woodstock, VT: Jewish Lights Publishing, 2003.

Haberman, Joshua O. *The God I Believe In.* New York: The Free Press, 1994.

Heschel, Abraham Joshua. *Between God and Man: An Interpretation of Judaism.* Edited by Fritz A. Rothschild. New York: Free Press, 1959.

Heschel, Abraham Joshua. *God in Search of Man: A Philosophy of Judaism.* New York: Noonday Press, 1955.

Himmelfarb, Martha. "*Sefer Zerubbabel.*" In *Rabbinic Fantasies,* edited by David Stern and Mark Jay Mirsky. New Haven: Yale University Press, 1990.

Hoffman, Lawrence A., ed. *Gates of Understanding.* New York: UAHC Press, 1977.

Hoffman, Lawrence A., ed. *Gates of Understanding 2.* New York: Central Conference of American Rabbis, 1984.

Holloway, Lynette. "A Spiritual Leader Lives On in Memory." *New York Times,* July 2, 1995.

Idel, Moshe. *Messianic Mystics.* New Haven: Yale University Press, 1998.

Jacobs, Joseph, and Moses Buttenwieser. "Messiah." In *Jewish Encyclopedia.* www.jewishencyclopedia.com/articles/10729-messiah. Originally published 1901–1906, placed online 2002.

Jacobs, Louis. "Franz Rosenzweig." In *The Jewish Religion: A Companion.* Oxford: Oxford University Press, 1995.

Jacobs, Louis. "Hermann Cohen." In *The Jewish Religion: A Companion.* Oxford: Oxford University Press, 1995.

Jacobs, Louis. *A Jewish Theology.* West Orange, NJ: Behrman House, 1973.

The Jerusalem Bible. Jerusalem: Koren Publishers, 1992.

Klagsbrun, Francine. *Voices of Wisdom: Jewish Ideals and Ethics for Everyday Living.* New York: Jonathan David, 1986.

Klausner, Joseph. *The Messianic Idea in Israel*. Translated by W.F. Stinespring. New York: Macmillan, 1955.

Knohl, Israel. *The Messiah Before Jesus: The Suffering Servant of the Dead Sea Scrolls*. Translated by David Maisel. Berkeley: University of California Press, 2000.

Kochan, Lionel. "Utopia." in *Twentieth Century Jewish Religious Thought*, edited by Arthur A. Cohen and Paul Mendes-Flohr. Philadelphia: Jewish Publication Society, 2009.

Landman, Leo, ed. *Messianism in the Talmudic Era*. New York: Ktav, 1979.

Lenowitz, Harris. *The Jewish Messiahs: From the Galilee to Crown Heights*. New York: Oxford University Press, 2001.

Levey, Samson H. "The Messiah and the Messianic Era: Jewish and Christian Perspectives." Lecture for the Evangelical Theological Society, delivered at Hebrew Union College–Jewish Institute of Religion, Los Angeles, 1970.

Levine, Robert N. *There Is No Messiah and You're It*. Woodstock, VT: Jewish Lights Publishing, 2003.

"The Messiah Issue." Special issue, *Moment* 37, no. 2 (March/April 2012).

Montefiore, C. G., and H. Loewe, eds. *A Rabbinic Anthology*. New York: Meridian Books; Philadelphia: Jewish Publication Society of America, 1963.

Patai, Raphael. *The Messiah Texts*. Detroit: Wayne State University Press, 1979.

Plaut, W. Gunther, general ed. *The Torah: A Modern Commentary*. Rev. ed. New York: URJ Press, 2005.

Reines, Alvin J. *Polydoxy: Explorations in a Philosophy of Liberal Religion*. Buffalo, NY: Prometheus Books, 1987.

Roskies, David G. *Against the Apocalypse: Responses to Catastrophe in Modern Jewish Culture*. Cambridge, MA: Harvard University Press, 1984.

Sandmel, Samuel, general ed. *The New English Bible with the Apocrypha*. Oxford Study ed. New York: Oxford University Press, 1972.

Sarachek, Joseph. *The Doctrine of the Messiah in Medieval Jewish Literature*. New York: Jewish Theological Society of America, 1932.

Scholem, Gershom G. *Major Trends in Jewish Mysticism*. New York: Schocken Books, 1941.

Scholem, Gershom. *The Messianic Idea in Judaism*. London: George Allen & Unwin, 1971.

Seeskin, Kenneth. *Jewish Messianic Thoughts in an Age of Despair*. Cambridge: Cambridge University Press, 2012.

Silver, Abba Hillel. *A History of Messianic Speculation in Israel*. Gloucester, MA: Peter Smith, 1978.

Sirat, Colette. *A History of Jewish Philosophy in the Middle Ages*. Cambridge: Cambridge University Press, 1985.

Sonsino, Rifat, and Daniel B. Syme. *Finding God: Ten Jewish Responses*. New York: UAHC Press, 1986.

Stern, Chaim, ed. *Gates of Prayer: The New Union Prayerbook*. New York: Central Conference of American Rabbis, 1975.

Stern, Chaim, ed. *Gates of Repentance: The New Union Prayerbook for the Days of Awe*. New York: Central Conference of American Rabbis, 1984.

Tanakh: The Holy Scriptures. Philadelphia: Jewish Publication Society, 1999.

Telushkin, Joseph. *Jewish Wisdom: Ethical, Spiritual, and Historical Lessons from the Great Works and Thinkers*. New York: William Morrow, 1994.

Treiman, Daniel. "Who's Your Messiah?" *Jewish Daily Forward*, January 3, 2008.

Urbach, Ephraim E. *The Sages: Their Concepts and Beliefs*. Translated by Israel Abrahams. Jerusalem: Magnes Press, 1987.

Vilnay, Zev. *Legends of Palestine*. Philadelphia: Jewish Publication Society of America, 1932.

Wiesel, Elie. *Souls on Fire: Portraits and Legends of Hasidic Masters*. New York: Simon & Schuster, 1982.

Wise, Michael, Martin Abegg, Jr., and Edward Cook. *The Dead Sea Scrolls: A New Translation*. New York: HarperCollins, 1996.

Yardley, Jim. "Messianic Fervor for Late Rabbi Divides Many Lubavitchers." *New York Times*, June 29, 1998.

INDEX

Adam 2, 3, 50, 60, 63, 73, 119

Akiva, Rabbi xii, 14, 41

Amidah 27, 72, 82, 110, 126, 137

animal xvii, xx, 60, 64, 66, 75, 89, 90, 122, 123

anoint/anointed 15, 20, 21, 22, 30, 49, 81, 106, 112, 124, 125

Antichrist 46, 54, 129

Antiochus 42, 46

apocalypse xv, xx, 34, 41, 42, 43, 44, 45, 47, 53, 118, 128, 132

apocalyptic/apocalyptics 14, 17, 32, 41, 42, 43, 44, 45, 46, 48, 50, 51, 52, 53, 54, 59, 80, 82, 92, 102, 108, 123, 124, 127, 128, 130, 138

apocalyptic battles/wars 14, 44, 51, 108, 128

apocalyptic literature vi, 32, 41, 42, 44, 45, 48, 50, 52, 92, 123, 130

apocalyptic wars/battles 14, 44, 51, 108, 128

Arbael/Arbel/Arbela 10, 44, 117, 120, 128

Armilus 45, 46, 47, 50, 54, 82

Assyria/Assyrian xvii, 4, 22, 23, 28

Av 3, 68

Ba'al Shem Tov/Besht/Israel ben Eliezer, Rabbi 12, 101, 102, 103, 139

Babylon/Babylonia/Babylonian xii, xvii, 3, 22, 23, 27, 28, 35, 36, 45, 46, 89, 127

Bar Kochba 6, 14, 35, 42, 46, 48, 49

Behemoth 74, 75

Besht/Ba'al Shem Tov/Israel ben Eliezer, Rabbi 12, 101, 102, 103, 139

Chabad/Lubavitch ix, 16, 104, 105, 106, 107, 112, 137, 139, 140

Christian/Christianity xi, 5, 13, 14, 41, 42, 46, 47, 52, 54, 70, 88, 99, 120, 124, 129, 132, 138

Creation 2, 3, 5, 7, 9, 43, 51, 58, 61, 63, 74, 75, 91, 92, 93, 94, 102, 114

Crusade/Crusaders xviii, 5, 6, 40, 100

Cyrus, King 21, 22, 23, 27, 33, 35, 125

Daniel 5, 34, 42, 49, 85

David, King xii, 3, 15, 19, 20, 21, 22, 23, 24, 30, 33, 35, 39, 48, 49, 50, 51, 52, 53, 54, 73, 75, 93, 110, 119, 120, 125, 127, 128, 130, 133

and descendants 22, 23, 24, 33, 48, 49, 50, 51, 52, 54, 110, 127, 128, 129, 130

and Messiah 3, 21, 23, 24, 30, 33, 48, 49, 50, 51, 52, 54, 73, 75, 93, 120, 128, 129, 130

reign of 19, 21, 22, 23

Day of Judgment 35, 85, 86, 136

Dead Sea Scrolls 42, 127, 128, 129, 130, 132

Deuteronomy 26, 38, 59, 126, 127

Diaspora xx, 20, 25, 27, 29, 119

donkey 11, 59, 123

Eden xvii, 60, 63, 73

Egypt 20, 38, 51, 53, 63, 68, 69, 102, 103, 120, 121

  Exodus from 63

Elijah xi, 3, 4, 8, 54, 73, 78, 79, 80, 81, 82, 93, 120, 122, 129, 134, 135

  in the Bible 54, 78, 79, 80, 120, 129, 134, 135

  and the Messiah 3, 4, 8, 54, 73, 79, 80, 81, 82, 93, 122, 129, 134, 135

Emancipation 10, 107, 108, 109, 110, 140

End of Days ix, x, 8, 41, 44, 48, 51, 54

Enlightenment 44

Europe xviii, 15, 27, 68, 102, 107, 110

evil 17, 33, 34, 36, 45, 55, 57, 58, 59, 60, 66, 75, 77, 85, 97, 111, 140

human evil 58, 59, 60, 66, 85, 97, 111

natural evil 58, 59, 60

exile ix, xvii, 7, 8, 19, 20, 22, 23, 25, 27, 28, 29, 30, 35, 36, 39, 41, 45, 46, 81, 82, 83, 84, 94, 102, 103, 106, 110, 127, 129

  Babylonian Exile xvii, 7, 22, 23, 27, 28, 29, 36, 45, 46, 127

  in Hasidism/mysticism 29, 94, 102, 103, 106

ingathering of the exiles ix, 27, 28, 29, 30, 82, 110, 127

Ezekiel xvii, xviii, xix, 44, 45, 46, 90, 137

Feast of the Righteous 72, 73, 75, 114

Gabriel 73, 85, 86, 138

Gehenna 86

gematria 5, 53

Gog/Magog 44, 45, 46, 55

Hadrian xviii, 48

HaLevi, Judah 5, 26

Hasidic Judaism/Hasidism ix, 8, 12, 16, 67, 94, 101, 102, 104, 105, 123, 137, 139

and the Messiah 12, 16, 94, 101, 102, 104, 105

Hasmonean/Maccabee 23, 35, 43, 125

Hephzibah xi, 50, 51, 52

Hezekiah, King 22, 23, 50, 73, 125, 129, 130

Holocaust 40, 99, 100, 105, 110, 121, 126, 139

humanity, messianic role of xx, 2, 10, 17, 94, 104, 105, 109, 110, 112

humanity, perfection of xx, 17, 60, 109, 110

Idel, Moshe 3, 93, 102, 119, 134, 140

Isaac xii, 73, 81, 83, 100, 133

Akedah/binding of 81, 82, 83, 133

Isaiah xviii, xix, 23, 24, 34, 50, 60, 66, 70, 74, 89, 98, 99, 100, 101, 125, 130

Israel ben Eliezer, Rabbi/Ba'al Shem Tov/Besht 12, 101, 102, 103, 139

Israel, Land of xi, xii, xvii, xx, 4, 14, 15, 19, 20, 21, 22, 23, 25, 26, 27, 28, 29, 30, 31, 32, 33, 36, 48, 59, 60, 71, 78, 80, 82, 90, 102, 103, 119, 121, 124, 125, 126, 136, 137

Israel, State of 19, 20, 25, 27, 30, 31, 32, 82, 105, 106, 117, 121, 124, 126, 127, 128, 134

Jeremiah 23, 28, 29, 68, 69

Jerusalem ix, xvii, 3, 6, 7, 14, 15, 17, 19, 22, 23, 30, 31, 35, 43, 46, 48, 49, 50, 51, 52, 53, 61, 63, 68, 71, 72, 85, 87, 89, 90, 101, 102, 106, 107, 109, 110, 117, 122, 123, 126, 127, 129, 134

Jesus 13, 14, 24, 119, 123, 129, 138

Joshua ben Levi, Rabbi 8, 9, 11, 122, 136

Judah xvii, 21, 22, 23, 28, 85, 124

tribe of 11, 49, 69

justice 2, 8, 9, 17, 33, 37, 49, 57, 65, 67, 78, 84, 86, 98, 109, 110, 112, 135, 138

Kabbalah 8, 15, 94, 102, 112, 113, 122, 137, 140
kabbalist 93, 102, 103, 122
Lurianic Kabbalah 15, 94, 102
King Messiah xii, 2, 11, 32, 53, 100, 106, 136
Klausner, Joseph 23, 24

Leviathan 74, 75
Lubavitch/Chabad ix, 16, 104, 105, 106, 107, 112, 137, 139, 140
Luria, Rabbi Isaac 94, 136

Maccabee/Hasmonean 23, 35, 43, 125
Magog/Gog 44, 45, 46, 55
Maimonides, Moses xviii, xix, xx, 6, 7, 17, 61, 62, 64, 65, 70, 91, 113, 137, 140
Messiah ben David 48, 49, 50, 51, 54, 93, 119, 128, 129
Messiah ben Ephraim 128, 138
Messiah ben Joseph 47, 48, 49, 50, 51, 54, 68, 104, 124, 128, 129, 138
messiah, in the Bible 21, 22, 24, 33
Messiah, birth pangs of the xviii, 39, 40, 44, 46, 47, 48, 50, 53, 57, 64, 85, 102
Messiah, in Conservative Judaism 140
Messiah, days of the 63, 64, 65, 78, 84, 132, 134
messiah, definition of 20, 21
messiah, false 6, 14, 16, 123, 126
Messiah, footprints of the xviii, xix
Messiah, in liberal Judaism 7, 110, 111, 112, 113, 141
Messiah, in Orthodox Judaism 121, 140, 141
Messiah, pre-historical 2, 3, 119

Messiah, suffering of 4, 11, 13, 47, 50, 98, 99, 100, 138, 139
Messiah, superhuman 33, 35, 36
Messiah, waiting for the xi, xii, xv, xvi, xvii, xviii, xx, 30, 115
Messianic Age xx, 2, 7, 10, 27, 29, 32, 33, 35, 37, 40, 42, 47, 49, 50, 60, 61, 62, 63, 64, 65, 67, 68, 72, 77, 79, 81, 84, 85, 86, 89, 92, 94, 108, 114, 126, 132
messianic calculation/calculators 5, 6, 7, 10, 13, 34
messianic era 140
messianic hope xviii, xx, 17, 25, 27, 49, 77, 109, 113, 116, 126
messianic pretender 14, 15, 16, 23, 124
messianic redemption 4, 17, 31, 63, 89, 92, 112, 128, 129, 134
messianic speculation 4, 5, 6, 7, 92, 106
messianic time 32, 92
messianic war xx, 50, 54
messianist 3, 5, 7, 37, 54, 60, 62, 77, 106, 107, 122
Michael 73, 82, 85
Moses xii, 20, 22, 25, 26, 33, 38, 41, 49, 50, 51, 66, 73, 74, 75, 120, 126
Moses ben Nachman/Nachmanides 60, 88, 138
mysticism ix, 8, 94, 97, 110, 112, 120, 137, 138
and messianism xx, 2, 6, 7, 8, 17, 29, 59, 61, 62, 68, 88, 91, 92, 93, 94, 122, 137, 138, 140

Nachmanides/Moses ben Nachman 60, 88, 138

Passover 5, 67, 80, 121, 131
peace xx, 2, 16, 17, 19, 36, 37, 38, 47, 49, 57, 64, 67, 78, 80, 81, 84, 87, 92, 93, 109, 114, 123, 141
pope 88, 123

Purim 67, 68, 131

The Rebbe/Schneerson, Rabbi
  Menachem Mendel ix, xi, 16, 104,
  105, 106, 107, 124, 139
Reform Judaism ix, x, 8, 17, 84, 107,
  108, 109, 110, 126, 140, 141
  classical Reform Judaism x, 8, 27,
    107, 108, 109, 110, 126, 140
  and messianism 8, 17, 84, 107, 108,
    109, 110, 126, 140, 141
  platforms of 27, 109, 126
repentance 9, 40, 41, 67, 83, 86
Resurrection of the Dead ix, 10, 35,
  70, 71, 72, 81, 109, 133, 135
Rome xviii, 6, 8, 14, 23, 35, 43, 46,
  48, 54
Rosh Hashanah 20, 83, 84, 121

Saadia Gaon 45, 71
Sabbath/Shabbat x, 5, 9, 12, 67, 80,
  104, 114, 135, 140
sacrifice 47, 81, 83, 86, 133
  ritual animal xvii, xx, 20, 66, 67, 89,
    90, 122
sacrificial worship xx, 109
Schneerson, Rabbi Menachem
  Mendel/The Rebbe ix, xi, 16, 104,
  105, 106, 107, 124, 139
Scholem, Gershom 54, 92, 93, 95,
  102
Sefer Zerubbabel xv, 42, 43, 45, 46, 50,
  51, 52, 53, 54, 68, 111, 118, 127,
  128, 129
Shabbat/Sabbath x, 5, 9, 12, 67, 80,
  104, 114, 135, 140
Shabbatei Zevi 6, 15, 68, 102, 124
Shechinah 29, 52, 62, 73, 82, 84, 103
shofar/shofarot 20, 27, 81, 82, 83, 84,
  124, 129, 135
social action/social justice 8, 98, 112,
  115, 138
social justice/social action 8, 98, 112,
  115, 138

Solomon, King 8, 20, 22, 73
Spain xviii, 15, 137
suffering, redemption and 3, 38, 39,
  40, 41, 44, 50, 55, 57, 86, 99, 127,
  139
suffering, vicarious 98, 99, 100, 101,
  139
Talmud xx, 5, 6, 7, 9, 12, 17, 29, 31,
  39, 40, 48, 55, 62, 67, 70, 75, 80,
  116, 120, 121, 130, 134, 136, 140
Temple, in Jerusalem ix, xvii, xx, 3,
  4, 15, 17, 22, 30, 36, 45, 46, 51, 63,
  68, 89, 90, 109, 113, 122, 127, 129,
  130, 137
Temple, Second xviii, 14, 22, 23, 26,
  35, 42, 43, 46, 48, 49, 66, 90, 127,
  128
Tishrei 5, 121
tzaddik/tzaddikim 104, 139

wine xx, 39, 59, 60, 64, 73, 74
World to Come 6, 62, 65, 66, 78, 133,
  134, 135, 136, 137, 140

Yochanan ben Zakkai, Rabbi 6, 134
Yom Kippur 15, 67, 83, 131

Zechariah 11, 49, 53, 127, 136
Zion ix, 19, 26, 30, 31, 109, 111, 126
Zionism 31, 127
Zionist 31, 140
Ziz 74, 75
Zohar 4, 5, 9, 52, 53, 61, 63, 74, 87,
  120, 132, 137

NOTES

RABBI ELAINE ROSE GLICKMAN is a noted teacher, speaker and author whose work includes the National Jewish Book Award finalist *Sacred Parenting: Jewish Wisdom for Your Family's Early Years*, *Living Torah*, *B'chol L'vavcha*, and *Haman and the Jews*. Her essays, sermons and poetry are widely published, and she is a featured guest on the syndicated television talk show *Daytime*.

RABBI NEIL GILLMAN, PhD, professor emeritus of Jewish philosophy at The Jewish Theological Seminary of America, is author of *Sacred Fragments: Recovering Theology for the Modern Jew*, winner of the National Jewish Book Award, and *The Death of Death: Resurrection and Immortality in Jewish Thought* (Jewish Lights), a finalist for the National Jewish Book Award and a Publishers Weekly "Best Book of the Year," among other books.

RABBI JUDITH Z. ABRAMS, PhD, is the founder and director of Maqom: A School for Adult Talmud Study (www.maqom.com) and a recipient of the Covenant Award for outstanding performance in the field of Jewish education. She is the author of *The Other Talmud—The Yerushalmi: Unlocking the Secrets of* The Talmud of Israel *for Judaism Today*, among other books about Talmud and prayer.

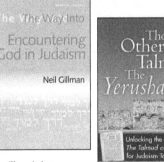